PUTTING SENSE INTO CONSENSUS

Solving the Puzzle
of
Making Team Decisions

by
Judy Ness
Connie Hoffman

"expanding your horizons"

VISTA Associates

PUTTING SENSE INTO CONSENSUS
Solving the Puzzle of Making Team Decisions

JUDY NESS AND CONNIE HOFFMAN

Vista Associates
5417 Orca Drive North East
Tacoma, WA 98422
(253) 925-1343

Published by **VISTA Associates**, Tacoma, Washington

Library of Congress Cataloging-in-Publication Data
Ness, Judy
Hoffman, Connie
Putting Sense into Consensus
ISBN 0-9665529-0-3

A Dedication

To our husbands, Arnie Ness and Vaughn Hoffman.
We thank them for their patience. There were many times
when our writing and editing took precedence over many of our family
responsibilities. We thank them for the meals cooked, the errands run
as we sat at our computers. Most importantly, we thank them for
their encouragement and moral support during those times
we wondered if the book would ever be finished.
Because of them we were able to do the
thinking and rethinking necessary to
translate our consensus model
to printed form.

Thank you Vaughn.
Thank you Arnie.

PUTTING SENSE INTO CONSENSUS
Solving the Puzzle of Making Team Decisions

TABLE OF CONTENTS

vi

CHAPTER 1

HELLOS AND HELPS:
SOME GUIDING THOUGHTS FOR THE READER

WELCOME! We are delighted you are reading our book. The content is the result of fifteen years working with groups, facilitating team decision making and evolving this practical wisdom on consensus into a practical model that teams could use to guide their consensus decision making.

Some of what you will read is the result of exciting breakthroughs as we were on the job actually working with teams and our intuition kicked in and gave us an insight or great idea. When this happened we continued to field test and refine the ideas until we were sure they consistently gave the results we wanted.

On the other hand, some of what you will read is the result of disaster. Often we were called in to help a team dig themselves out of a hole they were in because they had been using consensus poorly. As we helped them find their way out of the difficulties, we were careful to analyze their mistakes to determine how to help teams prevent such failures in the future.

In addition, some of what you will read is the result of our own mistakes. Occasionally as we worked with groups we inadvertently left out a key piece of the consensus puzzle. Again, we were intent in our analysis and evaluation of the cause and effect of the mistake so we could learn from the mistake and *fail forward*.

Another source of the content of the book is the well thought, difficult questions asked and real life situations posed for us by people in our workshops on consensus. This challenged us to deepen and broaden the development of our consensus model described in this book. We are genuinely grateful to those colleagues who "pushed for more."

Finally, much of what you read is the result of long hours in our office, deliberating about **why** teams use consensus, **what** is consensus, **when** to use consensus and **how** to reach consensus. This book has been long in production. We think the hours of writing and rewriting have been worth it. We hope you find this information as useful as we have. It is our wish that you enjoy reading ***Putting Sense into Consensus*** as much as we have enjoyed writing it.

The Organizing Metaphor: The Puzzle of Consensus

As indicated in our subtitle, *Solving the Puzzle of Making Team Decisions*, we have used the metaphor of a puzzle to organize and frame the information we want to share with you. The metaphor has helped us sequence and categorize the pieces of the consensus process. We hope it helps make the information more "user friendly," easier to understand as you read and more practical to apply.

Picture a complex jigsaw puzzle with all the pieces piled in the center of a table and the box lid complete with finished picture on a nearby chair. Your team has the challenge of putting together the puzzle. They must complete the puzzle in an efficient manner, in a reasonable period of time and involve all team members in the puzzle building process. This requires that they work collaboratively to examine each piece, sort out the corner and edge pieces and look for pieces that fit together until the picture is complete.

Reaching a decision by consensus as a team is similar to assembling that jigsaw puzzle. There are many pieces to the consensus process just as there are many pieces in the puzzle. There are corner, edge and center pieces in both. The four corner pieces in the puzzle of consensus are:

> **Why** use consensus?
> **What** is consensus?
> **When** do you use consensus?
> **How** do you reach consensus?

The answers to these questions form the content of Chapters 2 through 5. The questions are the corner pieces and the various answers are the edge pieces of the consensus puzzle. Together they form the border of the picture of team consensus. The center pieces are the varied process tools and process scripts that teams can use to reach authentic consensus decisions.

When building a jigsaw puzzle, the pieces are often sorted by color so a person knows the general location of the pieces. For example, blue pieces are at the top for the sky and the red pieces at the bottom for the tulip field. By sorting the pieces a person is more likely to fit matching pieces together. This is also true of the consensus puzzle. Some of the tools and scripts fit in the "What is consensus?" corner of the puzzle. Others with the "How do you reach consensus?" corner and so on.

There are other similarities between a jigsaw puzzle and consensus. Putting together a puzzle is fun and satisfying. It can also be a challenge to complete the picture the first time. Similarly, consensus is fun and satisfying when done well. Though consensus is challenging, teams become increasingly proficient in the use of the process as they practice completing the consensus puzzle, just as people assembling familiar puzzles do so more quickly and easily.

Beliefs about Consensus

People cannot successfully assemble a puzzle without a stable surface, such as a table top, to work on. The table top for our consensus puzzle is our collection of beliefs listed below. These beliefs are the philosophical foundation of this book.

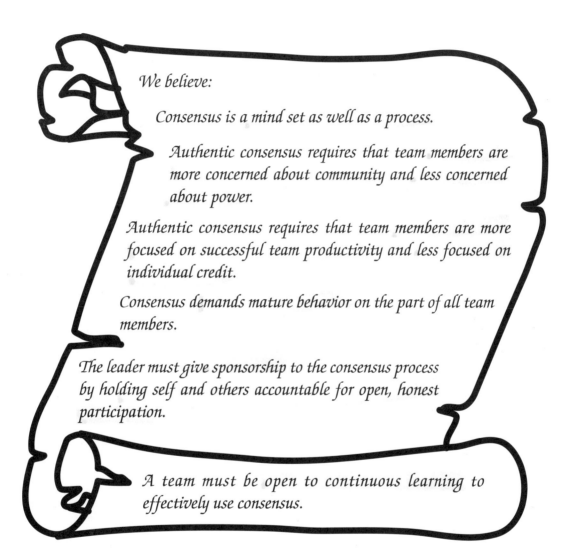

We believe:

Consensus is a mind set as well as a process.

Authentic consensus requires that team members are more concerned about community and less concerned about power.

Authentic consensus requires that team members are more focused on successful team productivity and less focused on individual credit.

Consensus demands mature behavior on the part of all team members.

The leader must give sponsorship to the consensus process by holding self and others accountable for open, honest participation.

A team must be open to continuous learning to effectively use consensus.

The more compatible you and your team are with these beliefs, the more this book will help you with the challenge and opportunity of *Putting Sense into Consensus.*

How to Read this Book

We value the time of the busy professional. We want the time you spend reading this book to give you the best possible results. To help this happen, we want to talk to you about:
- levels of experience with consensus
- cueing icons
- critical questions and key conclusions.

Levels of Experience

We realize that teams are at various levels of experience with consensus. Consequently, we organized this book so you can fit the content to your experience level. If you and your team are just beginning to use the consensus process, we suggest you start at the beginning of the book with highlighter and post notes in hand. Read chapter by chapter, becoming familiar with the content. Then reread the *Why* chapter and coach your team in answering this question, "Why should we use consensus?" Repeat the reread-and-coach approach for the *What*, *When* and *How* chapters. When your team can answer why, what, when and how they are ready to begin using the consensus tools in Chapter 6.

If your team has been using consensus but is experiencing difficulties resulting in team frustration and complaints, we suggest you scan the chapters in order, paying attention to the *Critical Questions* and *Key Conclusions* using a highlighter and post notes to mark the information you think will address the team's frustrations and problems. Reread these marked sections carefully and develop a plan for using the information with your team.

If you and your team are skillfully using consensus and you want to refine and polish your process, scan the book with highlighter and post notes in hand. "Shop" for ideas that will further strengthen your team's strong knowledge base and add to your collection of strategies. We suggest you pay particular attention to the tools found in Chapter Six.

Cueing Icons

You have heard it said that a picture is worth a thousand words. People's brains remember and organize information more effectively when visual symbols support ideas. Throughout this book we have used icons to provide important visual cues to point out the purpose and fit of specific pieces of information. We hope these cues will help you make maximum use of what you read. The icons are described on the following page. They are listed in the order in which they appear in the book.

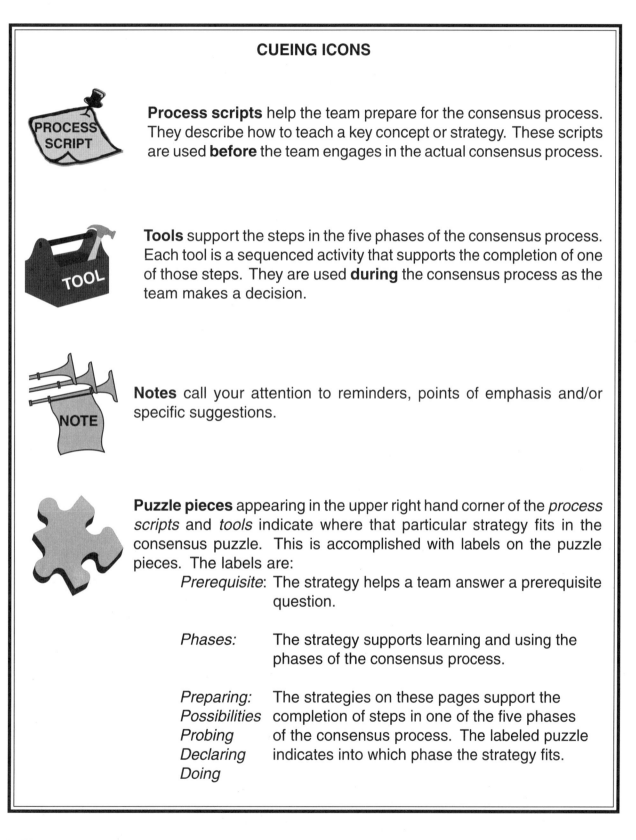

CUEING ICONS

Process scripts help the team prepare for the consensus process. They describe how to teach a key concept or strategy. These scripts are used **before** the team engages in the actual consensus process.

Tools support the steps in the five phases of the consensus process. Each tool is a sequenced activity that supports the completion of one of those steps. They are used **during** the consensus process as the team makes a decision.

Notes call your attention to reminders, points of emphasis and/or specific suggestions.

Puzzle pieces appearing in the upper right hand corner of the *process scripts* and *tools* indicate where that particular strategy fits in the consensus puzzle. This is accomplished with labels on the puzzle pieces. The labels are:

Prerequisite: The strategy helps a team answer a prerequisite question.

Phases: The strategy supports learning and using the phases of the consensus process.

Preparing: The strategies on these pages support the
Possibilities completion of steps in one of the five phases
Probing of the consensus process. The labeled puzzle
Declaring indicates into which phase the strategy fits.
Doing

<u>Critical Questions and Key Conclusions</u>
At the beginning of each chapter you will find *Critical Questions*. We hope these questions will serve as advance organizers helping you frame the information as you read each chapter. Then, at the end of the chapter, we summarize the answers to those questions with a statement known as *Key Conclusions*. It is our intention that these succinct summary statements will firm up the information contained in the chapter, helping you remember the essential concepts.

Before we write our next book we hope someone will create a non-gender word for the third person singular pronoun. We share the value of gender equity. We acknowledge the subtle and immense power of language. Thus, the word *he* should always be accompanied by *she* unless you are referring to a specific person. However, as we read and edited our book we thought the dual pronouns interrupted the flow. Consequently, we have chosen in most places to use *he*. We ask that you read *he* as representative of all mankind <u>and</u> womankind.

You now know the origins of this book, the organizing metaphor and our foundational beliefs. You also know how to match the book to your experience level, how to interpret the cueing icons, and the purpose of the critical questions and key conclusions. As you continue through the remaining chapters, we hope you find important answers, raise new questions, challenge some of your assumptions, affirm some of your values and practices and gain new knowledge and skills. We hope you are able to **put sense into consensus.** Turn the page and let's start putting together the consensus puzzle.

VISTA Associates
© 1998

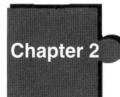

Chapter 2

WHY: A CORNER PIECE OF THE CONSENSUS PUZZLE

WHO ARE THE PLAYERS IN ORGANIZATIONAL DECISION MAKING?

WHAT ARE THE PAYOFFS FOR USING CONSENSUS?

WHAT ARE THE POTENTIAL PITFALLS OF CONSENSUS?

It is Thursday afternoon and team members are just leaving the meeting. Let's listen in:

"Can you believe it? Another top down decision! It's the same old thing - they decide and we do."

"All this talk of shared leadership and shared decision making is a real joke. I think what they mean is they'll make the decision and *share* it with us."

"You know, this is a real waste. If they had just asked us we could have pointed out how to avoid most of the timeline crunches. We could have saved all of us a lot of time and energy."

"Aren't we supposed to be a team?"

or. . .

It is Thursday afternoon and team members of a different team are just leaving their meeting. Again, let's listen in:

"Can you believe it? Another meeting! That must be the third one this week. I'm spending so much time at meetings, I don't have time to do my real job."

"Another three hours spent talking about trivial decisions. I don't really care what the decision is in this case."

"Isn't that why we have managers and supervisors? I thought they were paid those big salaries because they made decisions."

"Seems like not only do we have to make all the decisions but we have to make them all by consensus. I know we are supposed to be a team, but this is ridiculous."

Do either of these *after the meeting* conversations sound familiar? In these scenarios you see the two extremes of using consensus; the extreme of not using it at all and the extreme of using it too much. Clearly neither extreme effectively utilizes team decision making energy and potential. In either case, to continue doing what is not effective will result in a spiral of increasing frustration and team dysfunction.

The first thing your team must do to reverse this negative spiral is answer the question, "Why should consensus be part of our decision making process?" Answering this question involves understanding the changing <u>partnership</u> of players in organizational decision making, identifying the potential <u>payoffs</u> of consensus, and naming its potential <u>pitfalls</u>.

Partnership of Players

A pervasive responsibility in all organizations is making decisions. In the past, it was primarily the responsibility of the leader to make the important decisions for the organization. The person at the top decided what would and would not happen. In today's organization this essential activity has been significantly redefined and redistributed. Across the country, there is a strong trend toward flatter hierarchies resulting  in redefined roles and responsibilities for leaders and for team members. Leaders are expected to share the decision making authority with those they lead, to authentically invite them into the decision making process. This increased collaboration between leaders and team members may include gathering input, developing recommendations or making the final decision. *This partnership of leaders and team members in making decisions requires a clearly defined and understood process for making decisions by consensus.*

It is common sense and common knowledge that the people who must implement a decision often are the ones who most clearly understand the potential positive and negative implications of the decision. Thus, it is wise to use this knowledge by involving these team members early and authentically in the development of the decision. *This involvement requires skillful use of the consensus process.*

Complex decisions require the collective wisdom of the entire team. Bringing team members together so they can share their unique perspectives, experiences and skills helps utilize the diverse wisdom of the team and improves the quality of their decisions. *Complex decisions should be made by consensus.*

Why consensus? Because it strengthens the leader-team member partnership, ensures meaningful involvement of all team members and utilizes everyone's wisdom in making complex decisions facing the team. There are even more payoffs for consensus.

Potential Payoffs of Consensus

Higher quality decisions
When all perspectives are considered, when potential options are analyzed by a variety of team members, the resulting decision will be more likely to solve the real issue and be in alignment with the goals of the organization. While no one team member has all the answers, each team member undoubtedly has some of the answers. Consensus helps put these parts together for a better whole, a better decision.

Increased ownership of and commitment to implementing the decision
People support that which they help create. The opposite is also true. When a team is handed a decision that significantly impacts their work and they have had little or no opportunity to influence that decision, the decision remains external to them; a mandated *have-to*. Mandates generate very little commitment and this lack of commitment results in behaviors of apathy or sabotage. In turn, apathy or sabotage prevents successful implementation of the decision. Because those implementing the decision feel no real responsibility, their usual reaction is to blame those who made the decision for the lack of positive results. At the same time, the leader tends to blame the team for the failure of the implementation of the decision.

In contrast, consensus provides the opportunity for all team members to influence the decision. The result is a decision owned by the team; the decision is *theirs*. The decision is now internal to the team and team members acknowledge an increased sense of responsibility and accountability for successful implementation. If the decision made by consensus does not accomplish the intended results, the team is more likely to analyze, learn and problem solve rather than blame. The knowledge that each voice was heard and understood increases personal energy and enthusiasm. As personal energy and enthusiasm build, so does the collective energy and enthusiasm of the team.

Stronger and more positive team cultures
All teams function across the two dynamics of task and trust. Task defines what we want to accomplish while trust describes our interpersonal relationships. When a team makes decisions by consensus, there is a positive impact on both of these dynamics. Task is strengthened by higher quality decisions and an increased probability that decisions will be successfully implemented. Task capacity is thereby increased. Trust is nurtured by a growing sense of *we* and an increasing belief that individuals and the team have authentic power. Team members know they have influence. The trust level is thereby increased.

Why consensus? Because a team produces better decisions with increased team member ownership for successful implementation. As a result, teams are more productive and the trust relationship among team members is enhanced.

Potential Pitfalls of Consensus

Consensus has many payoffs, but the process is not problem free. There are potential pitfalls.

The tyranny of the minority

When consensus is not done appropriately it is possible that the voices of one or two team members can prevent consensus from being reached by the team. All it takes is for one person to say, "No, I do not agree," and to refuse to be influenced by other team members. This paralyzes the team, making it impossible to make a decision.

The tyranny of the majority

Another pitfall is the tendency for the majority to ignore the legitimate voices of the minority. Throughout the process it is essential that all team members try to hear and address all concerns. However, sometimes as a preferred option emerges, the team members in the majority become impatient and want to get on with making the decision. They become less willing to hear and problem solve the concerns of those who do not agree with them. When this happens, the minority feels discounted and even pressured to conform to the opinion of the majority. This is coercion, not consensus.

The tyranny of the clock

Though consensus is not quick, it is worth the investment of time for significant team decisions. However, many teams fail to realistically acknowledge the time required and plan accordingly. As a result they find themselves held hostage by the clock. They have to process their choices too quickly, rush the decision making process and often fail to establish a plan for implementation of the decision. The payoff for the team is less than satisfactory.

The absence of a skilled facilitator

Too often a team does not recognize the need for a skilled facilitator. They are not aware that guiding a team through consensus demands a clear understanding of the process and a rich repertoire of group dynamic and decision making strategies. They do not invest the necessary time and money in developing this expertise within the team. Without a capable facilitator the team will flounder because they:
- are not focused on the same issue,
- cannot differentiate between majority voting and consensus,
- have no means for tracking and displaying team members' opinions,
- cannot engineer full team support of a decision,
- do not have an action plan with clear assignments.

<u>Lack of understanding of key terms</u>

Without a common language of consensus and clear definitions of key terms, a team cannot successfully make consensus decisions. Mismatched definitions lead to mismatched expectations. It is as if team members were assembling different puzzles. Because they do not have a common picture, they try to put together pieces that do not fit. This wastes time, builds mistrust, creates cynicism, and invites sabotage.

Why consensus? Because when the process is done correctly the pitfalls can be avoided. Consensus can prevent the minority, the majority or the clock from making decisions for the team. With the help of a trained facilitator a knowledgable and skilled team can make high quality, positive impact decisions.

It is important to guide your team members in a discussion about the players, the payoffs, and the pitfalls. As a result they will have the answer to "Why use consensus?" This answer is a good beginning. However, critical questions remain to be answered if the team is to maximize their decision making energy and potential. These questions include:
- **What** is consensus?
- **When** is consensus appropriate?
- **How** do we reach consensus?
- **What tools** are necessary?

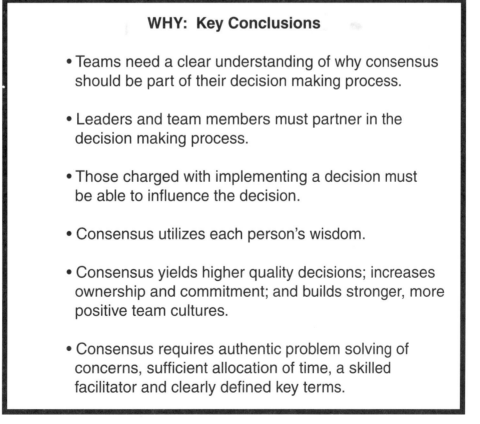

WHY: Key Conclusions

- Teams need a clear understanding of why consensus should be part of their decision making process.

- Leaders and team members must partner in the decision making process.

- Those charged with implementing a decision must be able to influence the decision.

- Consensus utilizes each person's wisdom.

- Consensus yields higher quality decisions; increases ownership and commitment; and builds stronger, more positive team cultures.

- Consensus requires authentic problem solving of concerns, sufficient allocation of time, a skilled facilitator and clearly defined key terms.

Chapter 3

WHAT: A CORNER PIECE OF THE CONSENSUS PUZZLE

WHAT ARE SOME OF THE MISUNDERSTANDINGS ABOUT CONSENSUS?

WHAT IS A SENSIBLE (UNPUZZLING) DEFINITION OF CONSENSUS?

WHAT ARE THE ESSENTIAL PREREQUISITES FOR SUCCESSFUL CONSENSUS?

HOW DOES A TEAM CUSTOMIZE THE ESSENTIAL PREREQUISITES SO THEY FIT THEIR UNIQUE TEAM?

At the Thursday meeting, after considerable time and heated discussion, a decision was made. However, as team members left the meeting, their comments indicated some serious confusion and discontent. Some of the puzzle pieces were not fitting together.

"I don't get it. We said this would be a consensus decision. But it wasn't. Not everyone agreed."

"Right! The decision wasn't what I wanted and no one even listened to why."

"I'm not even sure who agreed and who didn't. How do you figure out where people are if they don't say anything?"

"Sounds like I'm not the only one in the dark. We don't have a clue how to tell when consensus is reached. It seems to happen at some magic moment, and I don't have much confidence in magic."

"It's one thing to say we've made a decision and another for it to work. This wasn't my decision and I don't intend to support it."

Looks like trouble ahead for this team. There is obviously confusion about consensus. They do not seem to be clear about what consensus is. When team members are confused, that confusion often becomes frustration and resentment. This results in a poor foundation for making or implementing decisions. What the team needs is a clear definition of consensus. However, first they should examine some common misunderstandings about consensus and replace them with more accurate information.

Misunderstandings about consensus

There are several commonly held misunderstandings about the consensus process. When these misunderstandings influence a team's attempt to reach consensus, there is high potential for frustration and failure. It is essential that teams talk about the misunderstandings described on the following pages. We suggest you schedule some meeting time with your team and facilitate this conversation. The next few pages will help you prepare for this meeting.

Misunderstanding 1: Consensus means everyone agrees.

If this were a requirement for consensus decisions, few decisions would ever be reached and those that were would be of minimal importance. It is very rare when individuals on a team think the same way about issues of major importance. There is almost always a diversity of opinion. Consensus provides a process for hearing and honoring that diversity. Consensus makes it possible for a team to find common ground among these differing opinions and craft a decision that all team members can support. Not all team members need to agree with the decision, but all team members must give their support to the implementation of the decision.

Misunderstanding 2: All team decisions should be made by consensus.

Only those decisions of major importance and full team impact should be made by consensus. Before starting the consensus process the team should ask the series of **When** questions explained in Chapter 4. These questions can help a team sort the decisions that should be made by consensus from those that can be made using a different process. Other processes include majority vote, delegation to an individual or task force, and decisions made by the leader.

Misunderstanding 3: The final consensus decision reflects the first choice of each team member.

This is another misunderstanding. It is logically impossible that everyone will get his or her first choice. There are too many diverse ideas on most teams. Consensus is reached as team members consider a variety of options; with some they agree and with others they disagree. Everyone participates in problem solving the concerns people have with the choices they do not favor. As a result, team members often find they can support a choice they had previously found unacceptable.

Misunderstanding 4: Consensus is fast and easy.

Consensus requires skill on the part of all team members and one or more team members need to be a capable facilitator of the process. It takes time to learn the skills and even more time to become competent in their use. In the early stages of consensus decision making, it is easy for teams to get frustrated and give up. It may seem too complex and time consuming. Teams need to be encouraged. Remind them that the results will be worth the time and effort. They will realize higher quality decisions, increased ownership in the implementation of the decisions and enhanced team trust.

Misunderstanding 5: Consensus is compromise.

Compromise requires that everyone give up something and get something. Too often compromise results in a watered down option that is meaningful to few, if any, of the team members. When it is time to implement the decision everyone seems to be more aware of what they had to give up than what they gained and as a result there is usually minimal support for the implementation of the decision. In consensus decision making, the final decision is a reflection of considerable problem solving, rich dialogue and mutual influence. As a result, support by all team members is authentic.

Previously we suggested you schedule a meeting with your team to talk about the misunderstandings described here. When all the misunderstandings have been discussed, help your team summarize what they have learned by composing "Consensus Is..." statements. It is a good idea to record these statements on flip chart pages. Then you can use these pages as you periodically guide the team in a review of their statements. The review is especially important when a volatile decision must be made by consensus and/or when there are new members on your team.

When your team has replaced the misunderstandings with more accurate information, they are ready to study and truly understand a sensible, unpuzzling definition of consensus; a clear and workable definition that answers the question, "What is consensus?" This definition is one of the corner pieces of the consensus puzzle. It is an essential piece of information for the team wanting to become skilled in the consensus process. Turn the page for our definition of consensus.

A Sensible, Unpuzzling Definition of Consensus

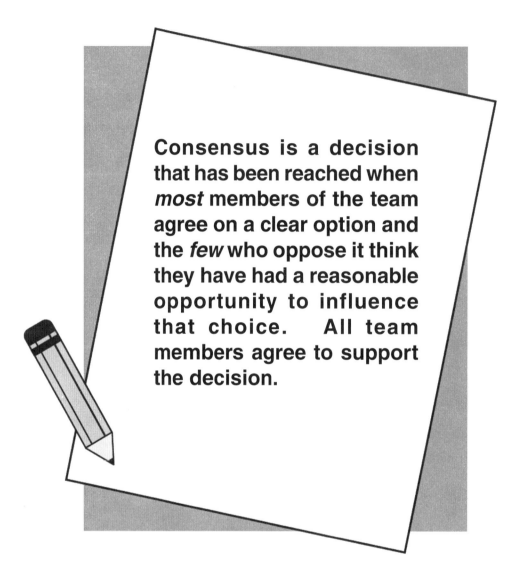

Consensus is a decision that has been reached when *most* members of the team agree on a clear option and the *few* who oppose it think they have had a reasonable opportunity to influence that choice. All team members agree to support the decision.

This straightforward definition will realistically ground the consensus process while still honoring the basic intent of consensus that all team members fully and openly participate in influencing the final decision. When this deceptively simple definition is authentically applied, the team can reach consensus both effectively and efficiently. They can avoid the tyranny of the *few* where one or two voices dominate or block the work of the team. In addition, the team can avoid the frustration of "undone" decisions, decisions that are not implemented because of insufficient support by all members of the team.

It is important for all team members to understand the definition of consensus. However, being able to recite it is not enough. They must also understand the prerequisites implied by the definition. The rest of this chapter explains these prerequisites.

VISTA Associates
© 1998

Essential Prerequisites for Consensus

These prerequisites are questions that should be answered by a team prior to using the consensus process. The questions are:
- **What is *most* for our team?**
- **What do we mean by *gifting* support ?**
- **What will our behaviors be with each other during the consensus process?**
- **What process will we use to reach consensus?**

Answering these questions requires time, energy and openness to learning on the part of the team. Because of this investment, there is a temptation to ignore the questions and to prematurely jump into trying to reach consensus. This is a serious mistake. Teams must ask and answer these questions.

The following information will assist you in helping your team formulate answers to these important prerequisite questions. The clearer the answers, the more effective will be the team's use of the consensus process because these answers translate into something specific the team must do to meet this prerequisite. As you read the answers to the questions you will notice an icon for process scripts. These icons reference an activity you can use to guide your team in meeting the prerequisites. Step-by-step directions for each process script are at the end of this chapter.

What is *most* for our team?
<u>*Most* is the minimum percentage of team members present at the meeting who agree or disagree with a decision</u>. Without this specified *most*, teams will waste time and energy trying to reach 100% agreement. If a team does not have a defined *most*, consensus is a vague and moving target. Time is needlessly spent arguing the question, "Are we there yet?"

If there is a *most*, there must be a *few*. <u>Team members whose opinions are different from *most* are known as the *few*</u>. For example, a team has narrowed their decision to two options. The team's specified *most* is 75%. It has been determined that eighty percent of the team supports option A. They are the *most*. The remaining 20% who prefer option B are the *few*. All team members need to understand the critical nature of these two concepts. Over the course of consensus decision making it is very likely that every team member will at some point find himself in the *most* and at another time in the *few*.

Reaching this specified *most* signals an important shift in the consensus process. At this point the focus is no longer determining which option has sufficient agreement. That has been determined. Now the focus moves to planning for implementation.

You will find a process script, **How Much is *Most***, on page 25. This process script helps a team determine their *most*. It is important to confirm that this *most* will stay constant across all consensus decisions. The team will always use the same percentage of people present as the minimum number of team members who must agree or disagree to say that consensus exists.

One other important point to clarify is that *most* is based on the percentage of people <u>in attendance</u> at the meeting when the decision is being made, not the total membership of the team. If a team has 40 members and *most* is 75%, 30 or more members would have to agree to reach *most* if all 40 members are at the meeting. If only 36 are present *most* is 27. Basing *most* on the actual number of members at the meeting prevents team members from blocking consensus by simply not attending the meeting.

On the other hand, being absent from a meeting does not have to mean a team member loses his or her ability to influence a decision. There is an appropriate way for an absent member to state his opinion. Some teams agree to accept proxy statements of agreement or disagreement on a decision. This has advantages and disadvantages. The advantage is people are not held hostage by their calendars. When they legitimately cannot attend a meeting because of calendar complications, they can still partake in the consensus process. Their voices can be heard. The disadvantage is that the person does not hear the dialogue that occurs during the meeting relative to the decision and this dialogue can greatly influence one's opinion of an option under consideration. When the proxy statements of agreement or disagreement are used, they should be in writing and be signed.

What do we mean by *gifting* support?
This prerequisite question has four answers:
1. a definition of *gifting*,
2. a description of support,
3. a description of sabotage,
4. a clarification of levels of support.

Gifting is a commitment made by each team member to consistently focus on the WE not me of teamwork. When *gifting*, each team member fulfills his responsibilities and respects the rights of his colleagues. These rights and responsibilities are nonnegotiable!

THE RIGHTS AND RESPONSIBILITIES OF BEING A TEAM PLAYER	
Rights	**Responsibilities**
• to be heard	• to speak openly and honestly
• to state my concerns	• to hear the concerns of others
• to have my concerns addressed by the team	• to participate in addressing all concerns
• to influence the final decision	• to be open to the influence of others
• to be treated with respect	• to be reasonable
• to participate in a complete and fair consensus process	• to be productive and efficient with our time
• to choose my level of support for the final decision	• to support the implementation of the final decision

Gifting has significant positive payoffs for the team. Decisions are more clearly understood by all team members and there is greater ownership of decisions. Successful implementation of decisions is more likely because all team members *gift* their support to that implementation. As a result of *gifting*, all team members participate fully and authentically in the consensus process.

Use the strategy *Gifting* **Support: Being a Team Player** to strengthen your team's commitment to *gift* support. This strategy is found on page 27.

Support is the act of doing my part to implement a decision that has been reached by the team. Support is being a team player. Support is easy to give if you are an advocate of the decision; if you are in the _most._ However, it is more of a challenge if you are not in favor of the decision; if you are in the _few._ The process script, **Defining Support**, helps your team build a common understanding of this critical concept. This process script is on page 31.

Sabotage is overtly or covertly interfering with the implementation of the decision. It is helpful if a team dialogues about sabotage and describes what it would look like and sound like. This dialogue helps team members know what behaviors are unacceptable. On page 33, you will find a process script for guiding a team in their unique description of sabotage. This strategy is known as **Cooking Up Trouble: A Recipe for Sabotage.**

Levels of support is a framework that allows team members to make choices regarding how much support they will give to the implementation of the decision. A person can give minimal support, moderate support, proactive support, or maximum support.

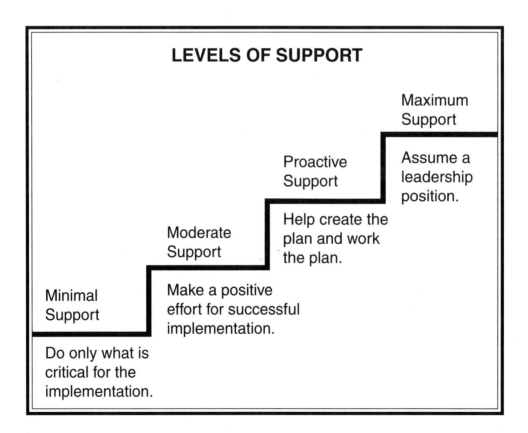

LEVELS OF SUPPORT

Maximum Support
Assume a leadership position.

Proactive Support
Help create the plan and work the plan.

Moderate Support
Make a positive effort for successful implementation.

Minimal Support
Do only what is critical for the implementation.

Team members must clearly understand they can support a decision at different levels and that they will be held accountable for meeting the expectations of the level of support they choose. To help your team members learn about these levels turn to **Learning About Levels: Different Ways to *Gift* Support** on page 35.

You now have the answers to "What is *most*?" and "How do we *gift* support?" There are two remaining prerequisite questions.

What will our behaviors be with each other during the consensus process?

As teams answer this prerequisite question they identify specific behaviors that will help create a climate of mutual respect, promote honest communication, and encourage authentic problem solving. These stated behaviors, often known as group agreements or operating principles, make it possible for the team to celebrate and reinforce appropriate behaviors as well as to name and problem solve inappropriate behaviors. To facilitate the development of a team's group agreements use the process script, **What's Right and What's Rude: Appropriate Team Behaviors** found on page 38.

What process will we use to reach consensus?

There is no ignoring the reality that consensus is a complex process that demands from both facilitator and participants professional maturity, well developed skills and commitment to quality work by the team. In the midst of this complexity, clarity is essential. The team must be clear about the consensus process. Otherwise, confusion about *how* to reach consensus may well be the pressure that causes a team to throw the consensus puzzle on the floor and declare the process impossible.

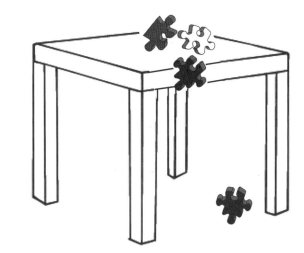

This final prerequisite question, "What process will we use to reach consensus?" is answered in detail in Chapter 5. As you read this chapter you will learn about the five phases of reaching consensus: **Preparation**, **Possibilities**, **Probing**, **Declaring** and **Doing**. Studying and using these five phases in the appropriate sequence helps a team know where they are in the process and what they should do next.

Having a clear definition of consensus and answering the prerequisite questions helps a team begin to make sense of the puzzle of consensus. The pieces of the puzzle begin to fit together.

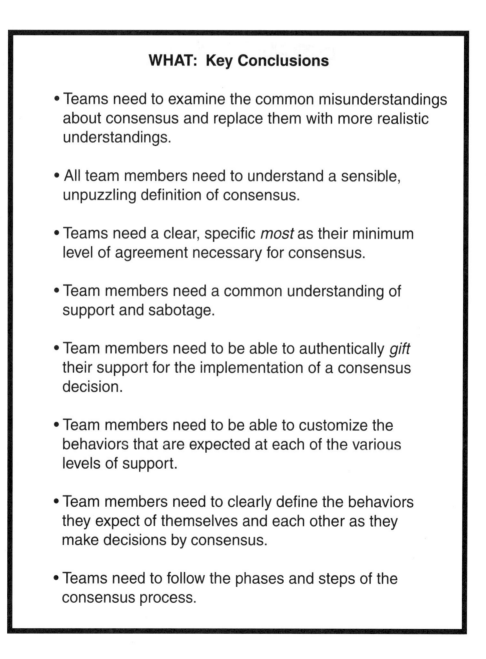

WHAT: Key Conclusions

- Teams need to examine the common misunderstandings about consensus and replace them with more realistic understandings.

- All team members need to understand a sensible, unpuzzling definition of consensus.

- Teams need a clear, specific *most* as their minimum level of agreement necessary for consensus.

- Team members need a common understanding of support and sabotage.

- Team members need to be able to authentically *gift* their support for the implementation of a consensus decision.

- Team members need to be able to customize the behaviors that are expected at each of the various levels of support.

- Team members need to clearly define the behaviors they expect of themselves and each other as they make decisions by consensus.

- Teams need to follow the phases and steps of the consensus process.

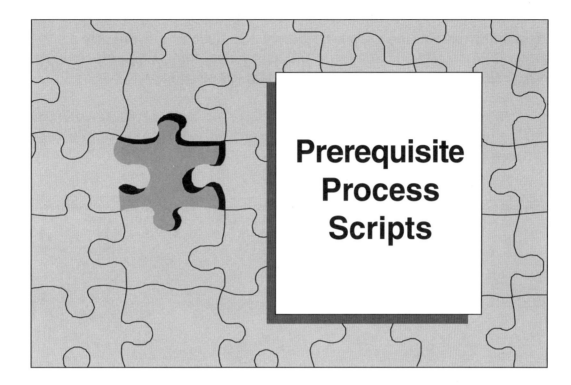

The process scripts on the following pages are designed to support a team as they develop their answers to the prerequisite questions. Every team has specific needs and a unique culture. Thus, some teams will want to use all of the process scripts while other teams will choose to use some. We encourage all teams to adjust the process scripts to fit their needs.

Process Scripts: An Introduction

On the following pages you will find process scripts that describe step-by-step strategies for helping teams answer the important prerequisite questions previously discussed in this chapter. When a team uses these process scripts they begin to personalize and customize their own unique answers to the prerequisite questions.

Each process script provides a facilitator with all the information he will need to guide the team through the process. Each process is scripted in a step-by-step format. We encourage facilitators to modify any process to ensure it meets the unique needs of a team.

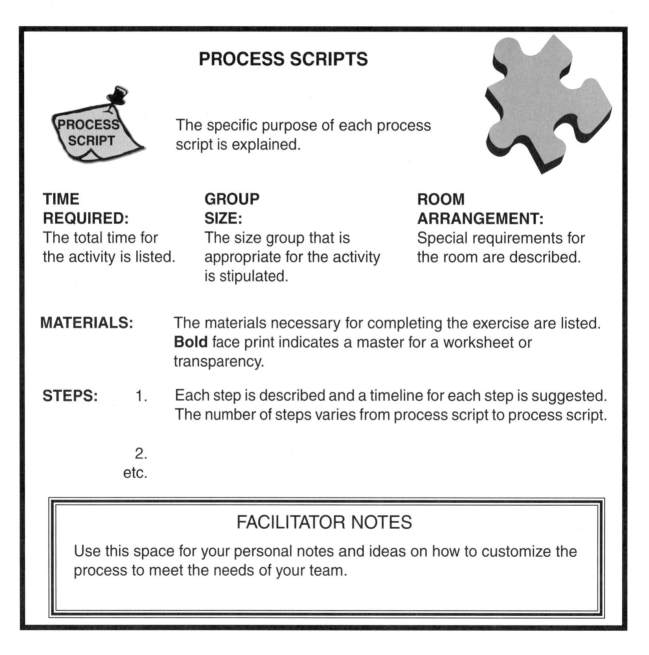

PROCESS SCRIPTS

The specific purpose of each process script is explained.

TIME REQUIRED:
The total time for the activity is listed.

GROUP SIZE:
The size group that is appropriate for the activity is stipulated.

ROOM ARRANGEMENT:
Special requirements for the room are described.

MATERIALS: The materials necessary for completing the exercise are listed. **Bold** face print indicates a master for a worksheet or transparency.

STEPS: 1. Each step is described and a timeline for each step is suggested. The number of steps varies from process script to process script.

2.

etc.

FACILITATOR NOTES

Use this space for your personal notes and ideas on how to customize the process to meet the needs of your team.

HOW MUCH IS *MOST?*

PREREQUISITES

The purpose of this process script is to establish what percentage of members at a meeting must agree or disagree with an option to declare that consensus has been reached.

TIME REQUIRED:	**GROUP SIZE:**	**ROOM ARRANGEMENT:**
45-65 minutes	Any size group	Tables for small groups and a place to post a wall chart that all can see

MATERIALS: 3 inch square post notes - 3 post notes per small group
Felt tip pens - one per small group
Flip chart page or butcher paper
Masking tape

STEPS: 1.   Clarify that for consensus to work, the team must define *most,* a minimum percentage of team members that must agree or disagree with a decision. Explain that the team is going to define their *most* during this meeting. Conduct a full team dialogue about the pluses and minuses of a *most* of 51% (simple majority), and of a *most* of 100% (unanimous).   10 minutes

Note: The dialogue should include the following points:

	Plus	Minus
51%	fast a common practice	potentially large number in opposition creates winners and losers
100%	everyone agrees everyone wins	very difficult to obtain results in watered down decisions

STEPS: 2.   Divide the team into small groups of 4-6 people in each group. Ask them to discuss and agree on a proposed percentage that would be *most* for the team. Encourage them to aim for the highest *most* that is realistic given the culture of their team. Specify that the nominations should be between the range of 60% to 95% in increments of five.

10 minutes

3.   Collect and post the small group nominations on the wall as a horizontal bar graph. (See example below.)   5 minutes

4.   Team members share the plusses and minuses for the different nominations. At the end of this discussion invite the small groups to determine if they have changed their collective opinion about the percentage they prefer. If so, they should fill out a new post note, go to the wall chart, remove their first post note nomination and place the new post note nomination in the appropriate place on the wall chart.

10 minutes

5.   Repeat this process until there is a clear preference. If no clear *most* is identified after two additional rounds, use the percentage with the majority of nominations for a trial period. At the end of this trial period this identified *most* can be reviewed and adjusted if necessary.

10 minutes per round

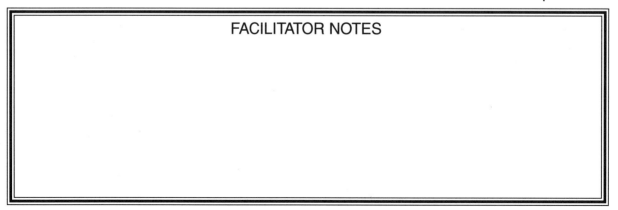

FACILITATOR NOTES

PROCESS
SCRIPT

GIFTING SUPPORT:
BEING A TEAM PLAYER

The purpose of this process script is to help the team clarify the conditions that constitute a reasonable opportunity to influence a decision, to develop an understanding of the importance of supporting a decision regardless of whether you agree or disagree, and to declare a commitment to give that support.

TIME REQUIRED:	GROUP SIZE:	ROOM ARRANGEMENT:
45 minutes	Any size group	Any room arrangement

MATERIALS: Overhead projector, screen and vis-a-vis pens
Flip chart
Felt tip pens
Definition of Consensus transparency
Conditions for *Gifting* Support transparency

STEPS:

1.   Show and review the **Definition of Consensus** transparency. Note in the definition the sentence, "All team members agree to support the decision." Remind people that this support is easily given if you have been in the *most* but is more difficult to give if you are in the *few*. When you are in the *few*, your support is truly a *gift* you give to the team.   5 minutes

2.   Return to the definition and focus on the phrase, "reasonable opportunity to influence." Point out that this "reasonable opportunity to influence" is a requirement if support is to be expected and *gifted*. Ask the team to describe what would constitute a "reasonable opportunity to influence." Record these responses on a flip chart page.   10 minutes

3.   Show the **Conditions for *Gifting* Support** transparency. Facilitate a dialogue comparing the information generated by the team in Step 2 with the conditions listed on the transparency. If any of the conditions listed on the transparency are not included in the team's list, they should be added at this point. Title this completed chart, "Our Team's Conditions for *Gifting* Support."   10 minutes

STEPS: 4.   Facilitate a team dialogue around the following questions:
"What happens to our effectiveness when a team member refuses to *gift* support even though the conditions for *gifting* support have been met?"
"How does this compare to sabotage?" "Does being a team player mean we are all expected to *gift* our support?"

10 minutes

5.   If the team agrees that *gifting* support is an essential part of being a team player, each individual publicly states his or her willingness to *gift* support by signing the "Our Team's Conditions for *Gifting* Support" chart.

If the team does not agree that *gifting* support is an essential part of being a team player, engage the team in a dialogue about whether or not they can continue to use consensus as a decision making method.

10 minutes

Note: The chart, "Our Team's Conditions for *Gifting* Support," will be used during the consensus process. It is helpful to create a permanent wall chart as well as copies for individual team members.

```
┌─────────────────────────────────────────────────────────┐
│                                                         │
│                   FACILITATOR NOTES                     │
│                                                         │
│                                                         │
│                                                         │
│                                                         │
│                                                         │
│                                                         │
│                                                         │
│                                                         │
│                                                         │
│                                                         │
│                                                         │
└─────────────────────────────────────────────────────────┘
```

**Consensus is a decision
that has been reached
when
most members of the team
agree on a clear option
and the *few*
who oppose it
think they have had
a reasonable opportunity
to influence that choice.
All team members
agree to support the
decision.**

Conditions for *Gifting* Support

I will *gift* my support to this decision. I have had a reasonable opportunity to influence the decision. I know this is true because:

- I have clearly stated my position.

- I have been heard and understood.

- My concerns have been addressed.

- I understand the decision.

DEFINING SUPPORT

The purpose of this process script is to ensure that all team members understand the concept of support.

TIME REQUIRED:

30 minutes

GROUP SIZE:

Any size group

ROOM ARRANGEMENT:

Any room arrangement

MATERIALS: Flip chart or overhead projector and blank transparencies
Vis-a-vis pens
Felt tip pens

STEPS:

1. Ask team members to pair up with one other team member and compare their individual understandings of the concept of *support* as they pertain to consensus decision making.   5 minutes

2. Write the word *support* in the center of a flip chart page or on a blank transparency. Ask people to share the ideas generated in their pair dialogue completed in Step 1. Record these ideas on lines coming from the word *support* in the center of the chart. This is commonly known as a mind map. (See sample mind map on the next page.)
10 minutes

   Note: If the group is larger than 40 use two facilitators and have one work with half the group in the front of the room and other with the second half in the back of the room. Invite each group to quickly review the mind map created by the other group.

3. Conduct a full team conversation about the emerging description of *support*.   10 minutes

4. Summarize the team's description of *support,* being sure that it includes the critical attributes of <u>each team member doing their part to support the implementation of the decision</u> and of <u>each person being a team player</u>. Note that this definition will be used by the team as they make decisions by consensus.   5 minutes

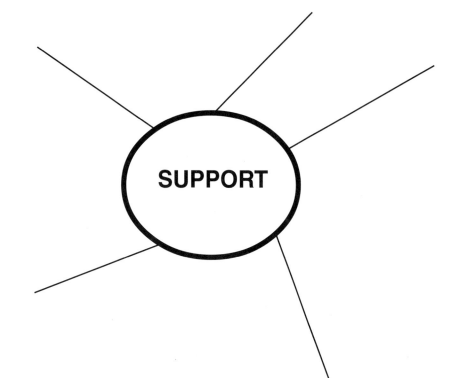

SUPPORT

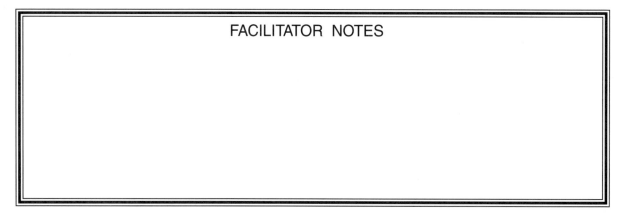

FACILITATOR NOTES

COOKING UP TROUBLE: A RECIPE FOR SABOTAGE

The purpose of this process script is to clearly name unacceptable behaviors that would sabotage a consensus decision.

TIME REQUIRED:	GROUP SIZE:	ROOM ARRANGEMENT:
30-40 minutes	Any size group	Tables for small groups and place to post recipe charts

MATERIALS:
Flip chart pad
Felt tip pen - one per small group
Sheets of 8 1/2" x 11" paper - one per small group
Masking tape

STEPS:

1. Divide the team into small groups of 4-6 people. Give each small group their materials as listed above. Remind the team that they have previously defined *support*. Now the team's focus is the opposite, to define *sabotage*. **5 minutes**

   Note: If the team has just finished the process for defining support in the same meeting, be sure you form new small groups with a different combination of team members.

2. Ask one person in each small group to share at their table a one word synonym or descriptive phrase for *sabotage*. Repeat for each person in the small group, recording all ideas on their sheet of paper. **5 minutes**

3. Ask the small groups to create a recipe for *sabotage* including specific ingredients (behaviors) and cooking instructions. Request they write the recipe on their flip chart page using the felt tip pen. **10 minutes**

4. Post the recipes. Invite team members to pair up with someone not in their original small group and "taste" the recipes by walking around the room and reading each flip chart page. **5-10 minutes**

STEPS: 5.   Conduct a full team dialogue about what they have learned about *sabotage*. Use the following questions as a guide:
 Which behaviors were consistently identified?
 What are the unacceptable behaviors for our team?
Chart the responses to these questions on a flip chart page.
5-10 minutes

Note: We suggest that the recorded responses from Step 5 are kept and posted when the team is making a decision or when they meet to review progress in implementing a consensus decision.

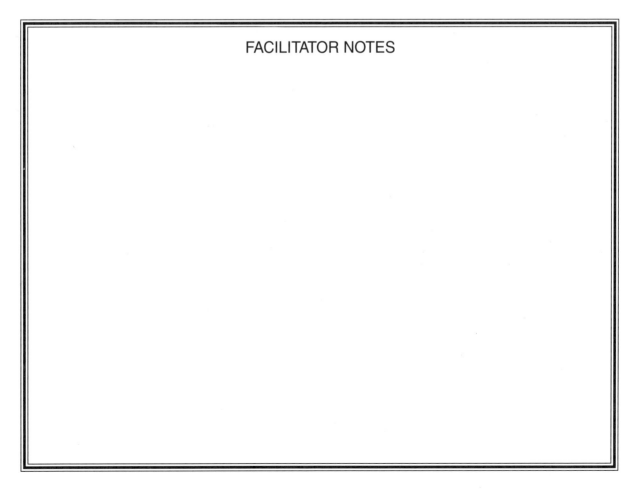

FACILITATOR NOTES

LEARNING ABOUT LEVELS:
DIFFERENT WAYS TO *GIFT* SUPPORT

The purpose of this process script is to name and understand the four levels of support and to clarify that team members can support a decision in different ways.

TIME REQUIRED:

20 minutes

GROUP SIZE:

Any size group

ROOM ARRANGEMENT:

Any room arrangement

MATERIALS: Overhead projector, screen and vis-a-vis pens
Customizing Support worksheet - one per team member
Customizing Support transparency
Pen or pencil - one per team member

STEPS: 1.   Prior to facilitating this process, use the **Customizing Support** worksheet as the blackline master to make a transparency. During this process you will be guiding the team in labeling each of the four columns. Each column represents a different level of support. The columns will be labeled in this order: minimum, moderate, proactive and maximum.   Prior to the meeting

2.   Distribute the **Customizing Support** worksheet to each team member. Ask the team to read the descriptors in each column. Focus them on the first column and teach the label <u>minimum</u>. Ask them to record this label on their worksheet.   4 minutes

3.   Repeat Step 2 labeling the remaining three columns: <u>moderate</u>, <u>proactive</u> and <u>maximum</u>.   6 minutes

4.   Engage the team in a dialogue around the following questions, "Why is it important to have different levels of support?" "How will these levels of support help us make consensus decisions?"   5 minutes

STEPS: 5. Point out that each time the team makes a consensus decision they will need to "customize" the levels of support. This means they will specifically define what is expected at each level of support. As a result, a team member who *gifts* their support at the minimal, moderate, proactive, or maximum level will clearly understand what he must do to *gift* that level of support for that specific decision.

5 minutes

FACILITATOR NOTES

VISTA Associates
© 1998

CUSTOMIZING SUPPORT

Decision

At this level of support a team member is expected to do only those things that are critical to the successful implementation of the decision.

At this level of support a team member is expected to go beyond the bare essentials by making an authentic contribution to the successful implementation of the decision.

At this level of support a team member is expected to advocate the success of the decision by helping plan the implementation as well as assisting in the monitoring and working of the plan.

At this level of support a team member is expected to support colleagues and to provide leadership in planning, implementing and evaluating the decision.

WHAT'S RIGHT AND WHAT'S RUDE: APPROPRIATE TEAM BEHAVIORS

The purpose of this process script is to identify specific behaviors team members need and can expect from each other during the consensus process.

TIME REQUIRED:	GROUP SIZE:	ROOM ARRANGEMENT:
55-65 minutes	Any size group	Tables for small groups

MATERIALS:

Blank puzzles of 12 pieces - one per small group
8 1/2" x 14" sheets of paper - four per small group
Felt tip pens
Masking tape

STEPS:

1. Order or create blank puzzles with a minimum of twelve pieces. Each piece needs to be large enough to write on. To order blank puzzles, call COMPOZE-A-PUZZLE, INC. at (516) 759-1101 or write the company at: 7 Littleworth Lane, Seacliff, NY, 11579.

   Prior to the meeting

2. Divide the team into small groups of four. Give each group one blank puzzle and four 8 1/2" x 14" sheets of paper. Ask the group to break apart the puzzle, setting the four corner pieces of the puzzle aside and distribute the remaining pieces to the members of the group. Each person will have two blank puzzle pieces.

   5 minutes

3. Pose the following question: "During the consensus process, what specific behaviors do you most need from other team members in order to be fully involved in the process?" Ask team members to think about what they need when they are in the *most* as well as what they need when they are in the *few*. Invite each individual to reflect and record on their blank puzzle pieces two specific behavior needs, one per puzzle piece.

   10 minutes

STEPS: 4. Instruct each small group to reassemble their puzzle, sharing with each other the behaviors each person wrote on their two puzzle pieces.   5 minutes

5. Using the behaviors shared in Step 4, direct each small group to identify four behaviors that are essential to all four group members. These four behaviors are recorded on the four corner pieces, one behavior per corner piece.   5 minutes

6. Invite team members to move around the room and read the behaviors recorded on the various puzzles. When they have finished looking at the puzzles, they return to their original small group.   5-10 minutes

7. Ask the small groups to write the behaviors from their four corner pieces on the 8 1/2" x 14" sheets of paper, one behavior per sheet of paper. Direct them to finish the following sentence stem as they record the behaviors on the paper: "We agree to . . ."   5 minutes

8. Facilitate the team in clustering similar statements together. This can be done in several ways:

> If the group is fifteen members or less, lay the sheets of paper across the floor or table tops. Ask team members to group similar behaviors.

> If the group is larger than fifteen, start with one group and ask them to read one of their four behavior statements. Ask the other groups to bring forward any similar statements, thus creating a cluster of similar behavior statements. 10 minutes

9. Hand out the clustered statements, one cluster per small group. Ask each small group to rewrite their assigned cluster into one statement.   5 minutes

10. Post the final statements. Lead the team in a discussion to determine if the statements are clear and reasonable. Continue the discussion until questions have been answered and concerns addressed. When the statements are declared clear and reasonable, they become the "group agreements" for the team.   5-10 minutes

Note: It is recommended that the team not have more than five to seven final behavior statements. This may require prioritizing and/or combining statements.

STEPS: 11.   The final behavior statements are transcribed and copies are distributed to all team members.   After the meeting

12.   Create a wall size chart of the final behavior statements. Team members sign this chart as an indication of their commitment to follow these guidelines. In many teams these guidelines are known as group agreements.   After the meeting

---

FACILITATOR NOTES

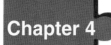
WHEN: A CORNER PIECE OF THE CONSENSUS PUZZLE

WHAT IS A REALITY FILTER?

WHAT IS AN IMPACT FILTER?

WHEN DO WE USE CONSENSUS?

It is Thursday and as usual the team is headed into their weekly meeting.

"Did you see the agenda? We'll never make all those decisions. Do they all have to be made by consensus?"

"I don't think so. There must be some way to decide when to vote and when to do consensus!"

Like many teams, our friends are struggling with when it is appropriate to spend the time to make decisions by consensus. They realize effective consensus cannot be rushed. They also realize not all decisions are equal in importance. They are increasingly aware that consensus should be reserved for those important team decisions whose implementation requires a high degree of support and commitment from all team members.

This raises a critical question. *How does your team know when consensus is the appropriate decision making method?* The answer to this question comes in two parts, **reality filters** and **impact filters**. **Reality filters** are measures of how practical it is to submit a situation to the consensus process by the entire team in order to produce a decision. **Impact filters** are measures of the impact of a potential decision on the team members themselves and on the work they are doing.

There are four filters in each category and they all can be phrased as questions. As you and your team focus on a situation that requires a decision, we suggest you answer these questions. The answers will help you determine if the decision requires consensus by the entire team or if the decision can be made by a simple majority vote or delegated to an individual or task force.

Begin with the four **reality filters**. Focus your team on the first question:

1. Does our team have the authority to make this decision?

It is essential that a team has the power to make a decision. Otherwise they may spend considerable time and effort in reaching a decision only to find themselves preempted by a higher authority in the organization. The result is frustration and cynicism. The next time you ask these people to participate in a consensus decision you will most likely meet strong resistance. Typically the leader is the best source for the answer to this authority question.

If the answer to the question is **NO**	If the answer to the question is **YES**
State who has authority to make the decision and organize so the team can give input or draft a recommendation.	Proceed to the next question.

2. Does the skill level among team members promote open communication and productive disagreement?

Some critical elements of consensus are hearing all voices, encouraging different perspectives and having an open mind. Authentic consensus cannot be reached if team members are unwilling to openly and publicly state their opinions during the meeting. It is equally difficult to reach consensus if disagreement and criticism of ideas are perceived as personal attacks. It is important for each team member to honestly reflect on his behaviors in these areas and for the team as a whole to consider their collective behavior patterns.

If the answer to the question is **NO**	If the answer to the question is **YES**
Facilitate activities that increase communication and productive conflict resolution skills.	Proceed to the next question.

VISTA Associates
© 1998

3. **Do we have a strong, adequate knowledge base about the situation requiring a decision?**

Quality decisions must be made by fully informed team members. Information must be accurate, complete and unbiased. Decisions based on "shared ignorance" seldom produce the results targeted by the team.

If the answer to the question is **NO**	If the answer to the question is **YES**
Delegate the decision to an expert or provide information to increase the team's knowledge base.	Proceed to the next question.

4. **Are we willing to spend the time required to reach consensus on this situation?**

As you know, consensus is not quick. Your team must be willing to schedule the time and participate fully during that time if they want to reach an authentic consensus decision. Notice the question does not read, "Do we have the time?" If a team is willing to spend the time, they will find the time.

If the answer to the question is **NO**	If the answer to the question is **YES**
Delegate the decision to a task force, the leader or designated team member. Hold a "Y'All Come" meeting.	Proceed to the **impact filter** questions.

A "Y'All Come" meeting is attended only by those team members who have a high interest in the situation and want to influence the decision. It is understood that those team members choosing not to attend agree to abide by the decision reached by those in attendance.

A *no* answer to any of the **reality filter** questions is a strong indication that consensus is not an appropriate decision making method. When a *no* answer is given, the team must either do what is necessary to change the answer to a *yes* or consider a decision making method other than consensus. When you have answered *yes* to all the **reality filter** questions, proceed to the four **impact filter** questions. The team should consider all the **impact filter** questions. However, they may be answered in any order. A *yes* answer to any **impact filter** question is a strong indication that consensus should be used.

Will the decision be long lasting?
Consensus is too time and effort intensive to use on decisions that will only briefly impact the team and their work. Determine the projected length of the impact for the potential decision. If that length of time is less than a month, the decision is not considered long lasting.

If the answer to the question is **NO**	If the answer to the question is **YES**
Consider a simple majority vote or delegating the decision to a task force or individual. Note: Don't forget to check the rest of the impact filters. A *yes* answer to any impact filter is a strong indication that consensus should be used.	Use consensus.

Will the decision establish or alter a priority goal for the team?
Priority goals require the ownership and commitment of the team if they are to be successfully accomplished. Therefore, establishing a priority goal or making significant changes to an existing priority goal builds a strong case for involving the entire team and using consensus as the decision making method.

If the answer to the question is **NO**	If the answer to the question is **YES**
Consider a simple majority vote or delegating the decision to a task force or individual.	Use consensus.

Will the decision change our way of doing day-to-day business?
Teams get into habit patterns and routines as they conduct their daily business. These patterns provide a considerable amount of security and predictability. Since making a decision that will change that pattern can cause initial discomfort and problems for some or all of the team members, it is advisable to give everyone the opportunity to influence the decision by using consensus.

If the answer to the question is **NO**	If the answer to the question is **YES**
Consider a simple majority vote or delegating the decision to a task force or individual.	Use consensus.

Will the decision significantly impact all the team members?
If the decision only impacts a few team members those team members should make the decision. We all find it frustrating to sit in meetings where the situation under consideration has little or nothing to do with our role or work in the team. An efficient team carefully considers which team members have a vested interest in the decision, ensures that those individuals have opportunity to influence the decision by being part of the consensus process and keeps other team members informed of the decision.

If the answer to the question is **NO**	If the answer to the question is **YES**
Consider a simple majority vote or delegating the decision to a task force or individual.	Use consensus.

Choosing consensus as the appropriate decision making method first requires a *yes* answer from <u>all</u> of the **reality filter** questions. If <u>any</u> of the **impact filter** questions are answered *yes*, it is very likely that consensus is necessary. Some teams may find it helpful to use the **when filters** flow chart on the following page.

WHEN IS CONSENSUS APPROPRIATE?

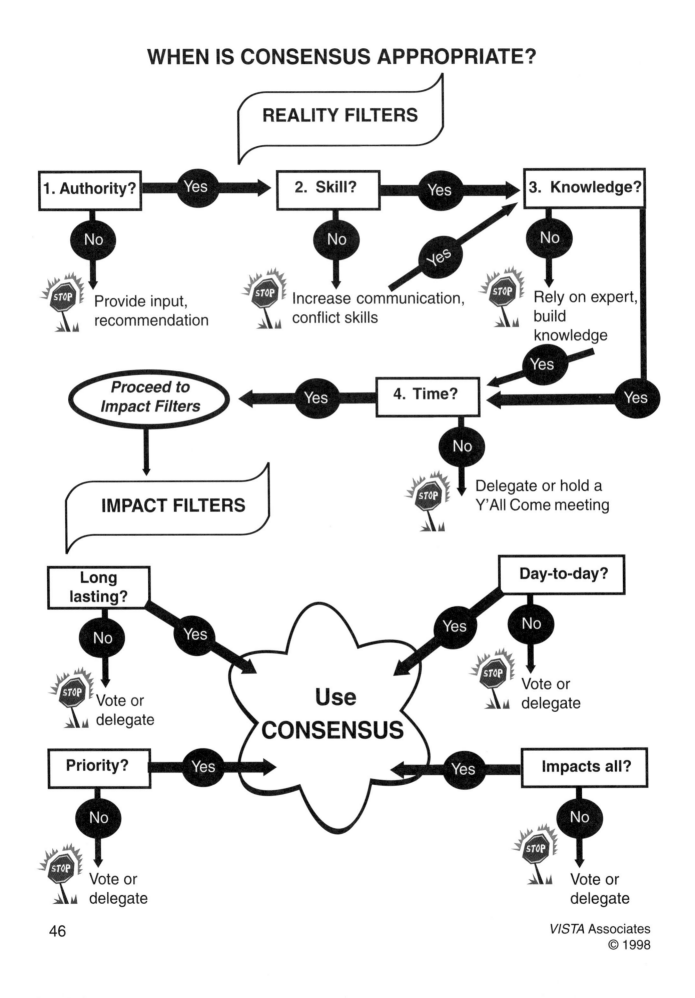

REALITY FILTERS

1. Authority? — Yes → 2. Skill? — Yes → 3. Knowledge?

No → Provide input, recommendation

No → Increase communication, conflict skills

No → Rely on expert, build knowledge

Yes → 4. Time? — Yes → Proceed to Impact Filters

No → Delegate or hold a Y'All Come meeting

IMPACT FILTERS

Long lasting? — Yes → Use CONSENSUS
No → Vote or delegate

Day-to-day? — Yes → Use CONSENSUS
No → Vote or delegate

Priority? — Yes → Use CONSENSUS
No → Vote or delegate

Impacts all? — Yes → Use CONSENSUS
No → Vote or delegate

The answers to the **reality** and **impact filter** questions will sometimes be provided by the leader. At other times the answers may require some team investigation and dialogue. With practice, a team can use the **when filters** to quickly determine whether or not to use consensus.

A concept that works for us is the 80/20 relationship of the Pareto principle. It is our experience that 20% of the decisions made by teams will consume 80% of the team's decision making time and energy. We urge teams to screen for those 20% by using the **When** questions. If the team has used the questions and received *yes* answers from all four of the **reality filters** and at least one *yes* from the **impact filters** it is a wise choice to use consensus. This is one of those 20% of the decisions that is worth the time and effort of consensus. It is very likely it is truly an important situation. We emphasize that this ratio of 80/20 is a general rule of thumb, not a hard and fast mathematical formula.

WHEN: Key Conclusions

- Reality filters describe practical conditions that must exist to choose consensus as the appropriate decision making method.

- Impact filters measure the significance of the effect of a decision on the team members and on the work of the team.

- Ask the four reality filter questions in order and if the answer to all four is *yes*, proceed with the impact filter questions.

- Ask the impact filter questions in any order and if there is a *yes* answer to any of the impact questions, consensus should be used.

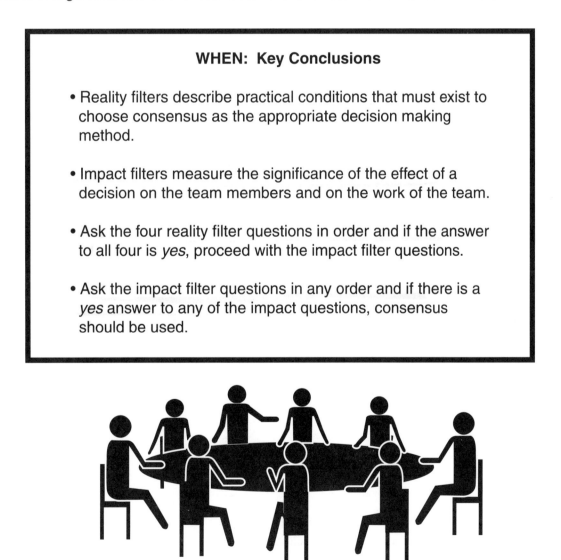

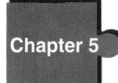
HOW? A CORNER PIECE OF THE CONSENSUS PUZZLE

> **WHAT ARE THE FIVE PHASES OF REACHING CONSENSUS?**
>
> **WHAT ARE THE SIXTEEN SPECIFIC STEPS USED ACROSS THE FIVE PHASES OF REACHING CONSENSUS?**
>
> **HOW MIGHT WE ASSESS OUR TEAM'S USE OF THE FIVE PHASES AND SIXTEEN STEPS?**

It is Thursday and the team has just finished meeting to make an important, complex decision. Let's listen in:

"Wow, we really got a lot done at this meeting! In the past we seemed to go in endless, hazy circles."

"This consensus process is really working well. We went from several options to a final decision that everyone could support."

"We've definitely shifted from blaming to naming concerns and problem solving as we make decisions. I know my concerns are heard and addressed."

"It sure helps to understand the rights and responsibilities of a team player."

"Reading that book on consensus is really paying off."

"I think I'm getting this. I think we are beginning to solve the puzzle of consensus."

Judging by this conversation, it's safe to say the team has made considerable progress in effectively using consensus as they make decisions. In previous chapters, they answered these questions: "Why use consensus? What is consensus? When should they use consensus."

When the team read the information in Chapter 5 they learned skills and information that helped them answer, "**How** do we use consensus?" Now that they understand and can use the **How** corner piece they are well on their way to putting sense into the consensus puzzle. Read on to see what they learned.

The steps of consensus are grouped into five phases known as the P's and D's of consensus: **Preparation, Possibilities, Probing, Declaring** and **Doing**. In the **Preparation Phase** the goal is to clearly state the specific situation that will be the focus of the team during the consensus building process. Team members clarify that everyone has the same understanding of the situation requiring a decision. Everyone is starting on the same page. During the **Possibilities Phase** they generate a variety of options or solutions to the situation. Members explore each option with an emphasis on gaining a common understanding. The goal of the **Probing Phase** is to "take the pulse of the team," to check individual opinions about the various options so they can eliminate and prioritize. In this phase the team also addresses concerns. In the **Declaring Phase** the team states the final decision they have reached and confirms that all team members will support the decision. Finally, in the **Doing Phase** the team plans and carries out the implementation of the decision. Effective consensus decision making by a team requires the intentional use of all five phases.

PREPARATION

POSSIBILITIES

PROBING

DECLARING

DOING

All team members need to understand and be able to participate in the five phases. The process script **Defining the Phases: Card Sort** gives directions for guiding your team through a card game that will help everyone learn a clear description of the five phases. This process script is found on page 62.

All five phases are essential for effective consensus. Teams need to **prepare**, generate **possibilities** and **probe** for preferred options. When one option is the clear choice of *most* of the team members, they need to **declare** the decision and **do** the implementation.

However, some teams require more details to guide their consensus process. They need more specific steps to follow within each phase. The remainder of this chapter provides those steps. You will find specific, sequential steps suggested for each of the five phases. The sixteen steps are not a rigid formula to be followed; rather they are suggestions for fitting together key pieces in the consensus puzzle. Each step is supported with a strategy know as a *tool*. You will see a tool box icon in the left margin naming the suggested tool for each step. These tools, complete with step-by-step directions, are located in Chapter Six.

PREPARATION PHASE

The goal of the Preparation Phase is to clearly state the specific situation that will be the focus of the team during the consensus building process.

1. State the situation.

Stating the situation involves naming the issue. This can be done by completing one of the following sentence stems. "Our concern is..." or "The situation is...." or "The situation that needs attention is...." This statement is now known as the *situation statement*. It is helpful if you write the situation statement on a flip chart page and post the page where it is easily seen by all team members.

If the team is larger than eight, they might check the accuracy of the situation statement in groups of three to four people. This allows all voices to be heard. If there is confusion or disagreement about the accuracy of the situation statement, this is shared with the entire group for clarification. All team members must agree with the accuracy of the statement before proceeding with the rest of the process.

Often teams struggle with lack of time and crowded meeting agendas. Finding ways to use time efficiently is critical. Consequently, a team might choose to complete Step 1 prior to the meeting. If so, the facilitator writes the situation statement on a flip chart page and posts it in a convenient location. Each team member reviews the situation statement and signs the sheet if he thinks the statement is accurate. If all team members sign, the meeting can begin with Step 2. If there are team members who are confused or disagree with the accuracy of the situation statement, they are responsible for sharing their concerns at the start of the meeting or for discussing it with the facilitator prior to the meeting.

 See **Stating the Situation: Group Memory**, page 69.

2. Clarify the situation.

Next, the team examines the information they have about the situation including who, what, where, and when in order to build a common base of understanding. They identify stakeholders who may be impacted by this decision. The critical facts are recorded on a flip chart page. If necessary, they do research to gather additional information about the situation. At this point, the facilitator checks to make sure all team members are well informed about the situation and understand the vocabulary being used.

Then, the team discusses critical parameters pertinent to the situation. These parameters are the boundaries within which they must work and might include the policies of the organization, law, contracts, best professional practices, etc. Clarity about these important items early in the process can prevent frustration and roadblocks later. It is a serious blow to a team's task productivity and trust level if they have completed the first four phases of the consensus process and then discover at the Doing Phase that their decision does not match one of the parameters. The leader of the team should be a resource for clear and accurate information about these parameters.

Finally, the team determines their goal. They clarify what they want to have achieved when they have finished working on the situation that is the focus of this application of the consensus process. Is it increased profits? Improved morale? Higher test scores for students? This goal statement can be a motivation for the team to keep persevering during the consensus process. It also serves as the basis for evaluating the effectiveness of the decision.

 See **Understanding the Situation: Critical Questions**, page 71.

3. Confirm the wording of the situation statement.

The team checks to see if the situation statement is still accurate. If so, the team moves to Step 4. If the discussion in Step 2 has resulted in a change in the situation statement, the new statement is recorded on the flip chart and the facilitator ensures that all team members agree on the new situation statement.

 See **Checking for Understanding: Confirming the Situation Statement**, page 74.

 The Preparation Phase is often neglected because teams frequently are under time pressure. The facilitator may need to convince the team of the importance of completing this step. It is critical for teams to remember that the better the preparation, the better the results. The better the preparation, the more efficient the process and the more effective the decision.

POSSIBILITIES PHASE

The goal of the Possibilities Phase is to generate multiple options or solutions for the team to consider as they begin to formulate a decision about the situation.

4. <u>Brainstorm options or identify predetermined options</u>.

The team generates *options*. An option is something the team could do that is likely to produce the outcomes they desire as a result of the consensus decision. If they have done research they try to develop options that reflect the findings of that research. Once the options are generated they are recorded on the flip chart. The team tries for optimum creativity and works to honor the rules of brainstorming included in the tool listed below.

There are times when a team is given a limited number of predetermined options and their charge is to decide which option is preferable. In this case, they skip Step 4.

  See **Encouraging Divergent Thinking: Brainstorming Options**, page 78.

5. <u>Talk about the options</u>.

The team members engage in a conversation to ensure that all participants understand all the options generated in Step 4. This is accomplished by clarifying terms, giving examples, asking and answering questions. It may be helpful to have each team member paraphrase the options. The emphasis in this step is on shared meaning through team dialogue.

  See **Promoting Dialogue: Compass Questions**, page 85.

 This concludes the Possibilities Phase. This phase is intended to get many ideas on the table. It is important to remember that this is not a time to evaluate ideas and care should be taken to invite ideas from all team members.

It is also important that team members understand that the first two phases, Preparing and Possibilities, open up and broaden the decision making process. As the team begins the next two phases, the team's agenda shifts to narrowing possibilities by analyzing and eliminating options.

Remember, if the group is larger than eight, they could work in small groups and then review each others' work. This allows all voices to be heard.

PROBING PHASE

The goal of the Probing Phase is to "take the pulse of the group," to check individual opinions about the various options so the team can eliminate and prioritize options.

6. Conduct position probes to prioritize and eliminate unacceptable options.

This step is intended to quickly eliminate options for which team members have little enthusiasm or support. The team analyzes and evaluates the options they have generated, removing those that everyone agrees can be eliminated.

See **Signaling My Opinion: Fist to Five**, page 88.
See **Displaying Preferences: Multi-Voting**, page 91.

7. Develop criteria for evaluating options.

All team members must have a clear understanding of the term criteria. Criteria is defined as a standard used to test the acceptability of an option; it is a principle used for evaluating an option. Consensus is more easily reached when all team members consistently evaluate options against the same principles. Lack of criteria may result in confusion and unnecessary disagreement.

See **Setting the Standards: Criteria Sort**, page 93.

8. Apply criteria to remaining options.

Now team members formally apply the criteria identified in Step 7 to each of the remaining options. As a result, team members will identify two or three options that are the best fit to the criteria. If they use the tool listed below, they will also have prioritized these options.

See **Analyzing Options: Option/Criteria Match**, page 99.

9. Conduct position probe(s) on remaining options and problem solve concerns until *most* is reached.

At this point the team considers each option still on the table at the end of Step 8. Using the tool listed on the next page, they determine how many team members support each option. Any team member who does not support an option states his concern and the team engages in problem solving to address these concerns. Probes are repeated until *most* is reached for one option.

Each probe should be clearly labeled as such so team members realize they are stating their individual positions, not actually making a team decision. With each probe the process used and the results produced should be recorded on the flip chart.

 See **Displaying Our Opinions: Levels of Yes and No**, page 102.

 Conducting multiple probes ensures that every team member has equal opportunity to authentically influence the final team decision.

An essential requirement of authentic consensus is clear differentiation between probing for individual position and actually making the team decision. In the Probing Phase the team is still exploring and members can change their minds. In the Declaring Phase the decision has been made and there is a shift to planning for implementation.

DECLARING PHASE

The goal of the Declaring Phase is to clearly state the final decision reached by the team and to confirm that all team members will support the decision.

10. Customize support.
During this step the team dialogues about the levels of support and customizes what *minimal*, *moderate*, *proactive* and *maximum* support will be for this decision. They clearly state what behavior(s) is/are expected at each level. They briefly review their description of sabotage and remind each other that these behaviors are not support and as such are not acceptable.

 See **Labeling the Levels: Customizing Support**, page 105.

11. Declare the decision.
When *most* is reached the facilitator indicates that it is time to "declare the decision." Team members now move from measuring individual positions to making the team decision. The facilitator states the option for which *most* has been reached and reviews the flip chart pages that document this fact. The facilitator conducts a final vote. This outcome is recorded on the flip chart. The flip chart page is labeled "Decision Declared" and dated.

 See **Declaring Our Agreement and Contribution: Commitment Continuum**, page 108.

12. *Gift* Support.

The facilitator reminds the team that since the consensus process has been authentically followed the expectation is that all team members will support the final decision. Team members who are part of the *most* have already declared their support for the decision. Team members who are part of the *few* (the minority) are asked to *gift* their support. To prepare for this *gifting*, all team members reflect on the following questions:

Have I fully explained my preference(s) to the team?

Has my preference been heard and understood by the team?

Has my concern been addressed?

Do I understand the option *most* support?

If the answers to these questions are *yes*, the team member is expected to *gift* his support. If the answer to any of these questions is *no*, the team member must share his specific concern with the team for additional problem solving.

The facilitator might assist a team member by asking, "What specifically do you not understand? What specific information have you not shared with the team? What specifically do you think has not been heard or understood?" When answers to these questions have been provided, continuing to repeat concerns is a nonproductive use of team time and energy. It is important for all team members to realize that being heard and understood does not mean others must agree with them.   At this point the facilitator declares that a decision has been made and states that the team will move on to the next agenda item.

See **Declaring Our Unity: Stepping Up to Support**, page 111.

In consensus the team must hear and honor all voices equitably but one voice must not halt the team from making a decision. After his voice has been heard it is his responsibility as a team member to *gift* support to the implementation of the decision. As team members become more skilled with the steps of the consensus process, support is more easily, honestly and consistently *gifted.*

DOING PHASE

The goal of the Doing Phase is to effectively implement the decision. It is essential to appoint a chairperson to guide and monitor the steps of the Doing Phase. This person is known as the implementation chair.

13. Develop an action plan.

A decision without an action plan may become merely a good intention. Thus, once consensus is reached, a clearly thought out action plan is necessary to implement the decision.   This plan should contain the basics:

- what are the action steps?
- who will do what part?
- by when?
- what resources will be needed?
- what data will be needed for evaluating the successes and failures relative to the decision?

When deciding who will do what part of the action plan, give some thought to the involvement of the stakeholders identified previously in the *Clarify the Situation* step of the Preparing Phase on page 52. The team engages in dialogue to determine which stakeholder groups need to be informed about the decision, which need to be involved in implementing the decision and which need to support the decision as it is implemented. Specific plans are made to support clear communication with each stakeholder group.

It is also important to specify the type of data that will be needed for the evaluation of the results of the action plan. The team specifies what baseline data they need and what benchmark data they need. The data is an essential part of the goal developed in Step 2. The team also decides how they will gather and analyze the data.

To save time, the action plan might be developed by a subcommittee. If so, the proposed action plan is reviewed and ratified by the entire team. At this point the committee double checks to be sure each person and/or group of people know and accept the responsibilities indicated on the action plan. This plan should be publicly displayed and checked periodically to monitor progress. Team members may need a "gentle reminder" about a part of the implementation they had agreed to do. This is usually done by the implementation chair.

   See **Developing the Details: An Action Plan**, page 114.

14. Implement the decision.

During this step individuals or groups complete their various assignments from the action plan. Progress on the action plan is monitored by the implementation chair and necessary adjustments are made. Throughout the implementation, concerns are named and addressed.

 See **Tracking Our Progress: A Wall Chart Display**, page 117.

15. Evaluate the effectiveness of the decision.

When the action plan is completed, the results should be evaluated. The team considers the evaluation data to determine if the goal set in Step 2 has been accomplished. They compare the benchmark data to the baseline data noting what has increased, decreased or remained the same. The team should also consider who needs to know the results of this evaluation.

 See **Evaluating the Results: Questions and Answers**, page 120.

16. Celebrate!

Effective teams celebrate their decisions; the good ones and the bad ones. The successes can be a source of energy for the team but the failures can be a tremendous source of learning. If a team is going to truly be a learning community, they need to be able to rejoice in their successes as well as examine their mistakes to see how they can be prevented in the future. This enables the team to *fail forward*.

 See **Weaving a Web of Celebration: Considering the Results**, page 122.

 Many a good decision has had poor results because there was not a plan of implementation. It does no good to prepare, generate possibilities, probe and declare if the team does not "do" the decision. The doing requires a careful action plan for its successful completion. The steps outlined in this phase will help guide that *doing*.

This concludes all the steps in all five phases. We strongly recommend that teams commit some time and energy to the study and practice of this information as they make decisions by consensus.

If you are a team member, we suggest you make an appointment with the leader of the team and share this information with him or her. Ask the leader to dedicate some team training budget and time to learning the phases and steps.

If you are the leader, share an overview of this information and arrange for the team to study the information. You will need to find budget, schedule time, designate a facilitator to support this study and be a source of information about parameters and authority for making decisions. As leader you should participate actively in this study. By doing so you emphasize the importance of the content.

If you are responsible for facilitating the team's decision making process, use this chapter to increase the *How* skills of your team. Set up study sessions and then coach your team in the use of the skills, strategies and tools.

When a team is clear about the steps to follow in reaching consensus, their energy can be more fully directed at the situation and they can take care to hear all voices, problem solve concerns, and generate the best possible decision. Time is not wasted, nor are decisions rushed or based on misinformation. When they gain competence in using the skills described, they approach consensus decisions with confidence and enthusiasm.

The consensus process is more interesting and accomplished more easily if the team has specific process tools to support the phases and steps. In this chapter, one or more tools were recommended for each specific step. These recommendations are based on our experience and each tool is fully explained in Chapter 6. However, teams are encouraged to be flexible and creative with how and when these tools are used during the consensus process. Over time each team will discover and develop additional tools that work well for them.

Learning to use consensus takes time and practice. We think a team should periodically evaluate their skill level and set goals for specific improvement. The form on the following page makes it possible for your team to quickly determine their areas of strength and weakness.

Make a copy of the form for every team member and request they fill it out. Tabulate and report the results. Celebrate the steps the team *always* uses. Then focus the team on the *sometimes* and *never* used steps and ask them to set one or two goals for improvement. Develop a plan of action to guide this improvement.

We suggest your team repeat the process in three months to determine if any progress has been made. Celebrate any accomplishments and then set a new goal for improvement.

How Well Are We Doing?

	Always	Sometimes	Never
Consensus is a multiple step process. These steps are grouped into five phases known as the P's and D's of consensus: **Preparation, Possibilities, Probing, Declaring** and **Doing**. Dialogue as a team and determine how well your team is doing with each step.			
Preparation Phase: 1. State the situation. 2. Clarify the situation. 3. Confirm the wording of the situation.			
Possibilities Phase: 4. Brainstorm options. 5. Talk about the options.			
Probing Phase: 6. Conduct position probes to prioritize and eliminate unacceptable options. 7. Develop criteria for evaluating options. 8. Apply criteria to remaining options. 9. Conduct position probe(s) on remaining options and problem solve concerns until *most* is reached.			
Declaring Phase: 10. Customize support. 11. Declare the decision. 12. *Gift* support.			
Doing Phase: 13. Develop an action plan. 14. Implement the decision. 15. Evaluate the effectiveness of the decision. 16. Celebrate!			

All teams should complete all five phases for every consensus decision but the size of the team will impact how many and how formally they follow the preceding sixteen steps. Small teams of eight or less will follow the steps very informally. They should keep a copy of this book handy so they can scan the steps at the start of the consensus process. As they finish each phase they can review the steps of that phase to be sure they have not left out an important element.

 Medium sized teams of nine to twenty should follow the steps as written. For teams larger than twenty, consider the following modification. The Preparing Phase is still done as a full team. Then a task force is formed and given the responsibility to prepare a proposal. To prepare the proposal the task force will use the **Forming a Proposal: Straw Draft** strategy. This tool is found in Chapter Six, page 76 as a variation in the Preparing phase.

HOW: Key Conclusions

- Teams need to learn and consistently use a clear step-by-step process for reaching consensus.

- A team prepares for consensus by making sure that all team members are focused on the same situation and have a common understanding of what the situation involves.

- Quality decisions result from considering multiple possibilities.

- It is important to conduct multiple probes to determine individual opinions and concerns.

- The team has a responsibility to problem solve concerns.

- When *most* is reached, the team needs to clearly declare the decision.

- Each individual has a responsibility to *gift* support.

- The team needs solid action plans to implement the decision.

DEFINING THE PHASES: CARD SORT

PHASES

The purpose of this process script is to help team members sequence and describe the five phases of the consensus process. This can be an introduction or a review of the five phases.

TIME REQUIRED:	**GROUP SIZE:**	**ROOM ARRANGEMENT:**
40-50 minutes	Any size group	Tables and chairs arranged so people are in groups of six

MATERIALS:
Five Phases Cards - one set per small group
Five Phases Card Game master - one per small group
One sheet of paper and pen per small group
Five Phases transparency
Overhead projector and screen
Sheet of paper to cover the transparency

STEPS:

1. Before the session, run one copy of the **Five Phases Card Game** master for each group of six people. Use card stock paper. Cut on the dotted lines to create a set of ten cards. Bind each set of cards with a rubber band. *Prior to meeting*

2. Divide people into groups of six. Then give one set of **Five Phases Cards** to each small group. *5 minutes*

3. Appoint a person to serve as the small group leader. Request that person to place all cards print side up on the table so all members of the small group can see the cards. *2 minutes*

4. Instruct the small groups to sort the labels of the phases from the descriptions. *3 minutes*

5. Ask them to sequence the five phases. *5 minutes*

6. Place the **Five Phases** transparency on the overhead, cover it with a sheet of paper and turn on the overhead. Ask the full group to name the first phase, then pull down the paper and reveal the word *Preparing*. Invite groups to correct their sequence if they have made

STEPS: 6. an error. Continue this reveal process until all phases have been
(cont'd) named in sequence. Usually people can easily sequence the phases
as there is a natural logic to them. Point this out to the full group.

5 minutes

7. Direct the small groups' attention to the description cards and ask
them to match descriptions with labels. 5 minutes

8. Distribute an uncut copy of the **Five Phase Card Game** to each small
group. Ask them to check the accuracy of their matches and make
the necessary corrections. 5 minutes

9. Invite them to discuss the descriptions and note any questions.
Request that the table leader record these questions. 10 minutes

10. If time permits, conduct a full team discussion to answer the questions
from the small groups. If not, collect the questions and prepare written
answers to be distributed to all team members. 10 minutes

FACILITATOR NOTES:

Preparing	**Goal:** Clearly state the situation that is the focus of the consensus process.
Possibilities	**Goal:** Generate and explore multiple options.
Probing	**Goal:** Check people's opinions about various options to eliminate and prioritize options.
Declaring	**Goal:** Clearly state the final decision and confirm support of all team members.
Doing	**Goal:** Plan for and carry out the implementation of the decision.

HOW: Phases in the Consensus Process

Five Phases:

☆**Preparing**

☆**Possibilities**

☆**Probing**

☆**Declaring**

☆**Doing**

CHAPTER 6

PROCESS TOOLS: FILLING IN THE PUZZLE

WHAT IS A PROCESS TOOL?

HOW IS A PROCESS TOOL DIFFERENT FROM A PROCESS SCRIPT?

HOW DO THE TOOLS MATCH UP WITH THE STEPS?

DO WE HAVE TO USE ALL THE TOOLS?

In the previous chapters you worked on the four corner pieces of the consensus puzzle. You considered the questions:

Why use consensus?
What is consensus?
When should consensus be used?
How do we reach consensus?

The answers to these questions served as the edge pieces and now our consensus puzzle has a complete border. You even put some interior pieces into the puzzle as you examined the prerequisite process scripts. These process scripts were step-by-step activities designed to help prepare your team for effective use of the consensus process.

In this chapter you will fill in almost all of the remaining pieces. Each piece is a process tool that provides sequenced directions to support the successful completion of a step in one of the five phases of the consensus process. There is at least one tool for each of the sixteen steps.

Not all teams will choose to use all the tools. We suggest you scan the tools and select those that fit the needs of your team. After studying the tool of your choice, guide your team in its application.

Space is provided at the end of each tool for facilitator notes. We suggest you use this space to customize the tools so they match the culture and learning style of your team.

On the next page you will find a Table of Contents listing all of the tools.

PROCESS TOOLS: FILLING IN THE PUZZLE

STATING THE SITUATION: GROUP MEMORY

The purpose of this tool is to provide a visible, written statement that clearly states the situation on which the team will be working as they make a decision.

TIME REQUIRED:

Ongoing throughout the meeting, times vary depending on option chosen

GROUP SIZE:

Any size group

ROOM ARRANGEMENT:

All team members must be able to easily see the flip chart pages.

MATERIALS: Flip chart
Felt tip pens

STEP: 1.   Facilitate a team dialogue to identify the situation on which they are to work. The team can only work on one situation at a time and it is essential that all team members are focused on the same situation. This can be accomplished by doing one of the following:

OPTIONS: a. Write a statement of the situation on a flip chart which is positioned where all team members can easily see it. This flip chart is used throughout the consensus process and is known as the group memory. Lead a team dialogue about the situation statement making sure that team members agree it is accurate and clear. Check to see if all team members can paraphrase the situation statement.   5-10 minutes

b. Each team member writes their understanding of the situation in a one sentence statement. These statements are shared. Key words and phrases are recorded on the group memory. The team identifies patterns across these key words and phrases and uses these as a guide for writing a situation statement. Next, lead a team dialogue to make sure this situation statement is both accurate and clear. Check to see if all team members can paraphrase the situation statement.   10-15 minutes

OPTIONS:
(cont'd)

Note: If the team is larger than 30, organize team members into groups of six. Each group records key words and phrases on a sheet of flip chart paper and these sheets are posted. Guide the full team in identifying patterns from these sheets and help the team use these patterns to develop the situation statement.

c. State the situation and write this situation statement on a flip chart page. Lead a full team dialogue about the situation to make sure the statement is clearly understood. Check to see that all team members can paraphrase the situation statement.

5-10 minutes

The completed situation statement is posted where it can easily be seen so the team can refer to it throughout the rest of the consensus process.

Note: For more information about additional uses of the group memory see *Chapter 7: Tips and Hints: Supporting the Process.*

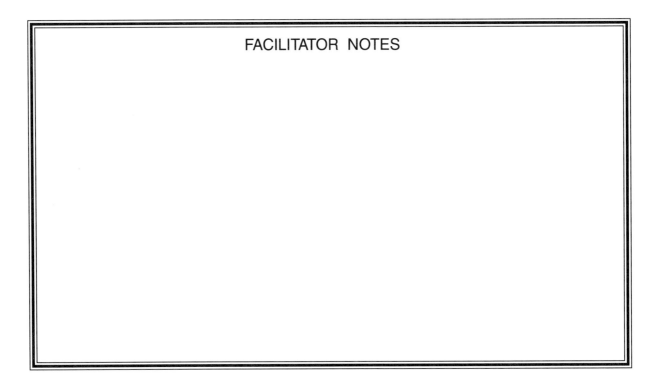

FACILITATOR NOTES

UNDERSTANDING THE SITUATION: CRITICAL QUESTIONS

The purpose of this tool is to help the team explore the issue and build a common base of knowledge before attempting to generate options.

TIME REQUIRED:	**GROUP SIZE:**	**ROOM ARRANGEMENT:**
15-60 minutes depending on number of questions explored	Any size group	All team members must be able to easily see the posted flip chart pages.

MATERIALS: Flip chart
Felt tip pens
Masking tape
Critical Questions: A Menu Page

STEPS:

1. Review the **Critical Questions Menu Page** and determine which critical question or questions the team will use as they explore the issue. Record these questions, one per flip chart page.

   Prior to the start of the meeting

2. Write the situation statement on a flip chart page and clarify that all members of the team understand and are prepared to explore this issue. Focus the team on the first question identified in Step 1 and facilitate a team dialogue about this question as it relates to the focus issue. Record comments on the flip chart page.   *5-10 minutes*

3. Repeat Step 2 with the next critical question. Work through each critical question, recording and posting team members' thoughts.

   5-10 minutes per question

4. Ask the team what conclusions they can draw based on the information shared by exploring the critical question(s).   Determine if the team thinks they should continue to work on the situation. If so, move on to the next step in the Preparing Phase. If not, determine what additional information is needed or what the team believes their next step should be relative to the situation.   *5 minutes*

VARIATION: If the group is larger than 10 members, consider dividing the total team into smaller groups of 5-6 people in a group. Assign each group one of the critical questions. Each group dialogues about the question, records their thoughts on the flip chart page and shares their thoughts with the total team in one of the following ways:
- post their chart and take turns sharing a verbal summary,
- post their chart and then provide time to move around the room reading each other's charts,
- pass their chart on to another small group who reviews it and adds additional thoughts; continue passing charts until all charts have been reviewed.

Note: The team may want to determine which critical questions they will use to explore the issue. If so, you will need to provide additional time at the beginning of the process for the question selection.

FACILITATOR NOTES

CRITICAL QUESTIONS: A MENU PAGE

Gaining Perspective on the Situation:

<u>Priority</u>: Is this situation important? Why? Why not?

<u>Urgency</u>: Does this situation demand attention now? Why? Why not?

<u>Ownership</u>: Whose problem is it? Are we motivated to work on this situation? Why? Why not? Do we have a choice?

If the situation is not a priority, the team may want to set it aside, table it until another time or delegate it to another task force or individual.

If the team has no ownership, they delegate the situation to a task force or individual or they may also explore expanding the membership of the team to include those with more interest in working on the situation.

Considering Potential Causes:

- Is the situation the result of working relationships, a problem with how people work together? ***Interpersonal cause***

- Is the situation a result of how we are organized, a problem of authority levels, reporting and supervision patterns, connections with others within the organization but external to our team? ***System cause***

- Is the situation a result of lack of training, development of skills, knowledge, coaching, or learning? ***Competency cause***

- Is the situation a result of insufficient or poor use of time, materials, money, or people? ***Resource cause***

- Is the situation a result of values, habits, traditions, or group norms? ***Culture cause***

- Is the situation a result of inaccurate, missing, incomplete, or inconsistent information? ***Communication cause***

Conducting a Journalistic Investigation:

<u>Who</u>	Who is involved? Who will be impacted?
<u>What</u>	What are we currently doing? What are the causes? What do we need to know?
<u>When</u>	When does this situation occur? When do we have to have a solution and/or plan? How long has this been a situation?
<u>Where</u>	Where does this situation happen? (physical location or at some point in a process)
<u>Why</u>	Why is this happening?

CHECKING FOR UNDERSTANDING: CONFIRMING THE SITUATION STATEMENT

The purpose of this tool is to revisit the original situation statement and affirm that the situation statement is still accurate considering what the team has learned through their previous dialogue and experiences.

TIME REQUIRED:

15-25 minutes

GROUP SIZE:

Any size group

ROOM ARRANGEMENT:

All team members must be able to see the posted flip chart page and easily hear each other.

MATERIALS: Flip chart
Felt tip pens
Blank paper - one sheet per team member

STEPS:

1. Focus the team on the original situation statement as recorded in the group memory. The group memory is the flip chart used in the tool, Stating the Situation: Group Memory on page 69. Quickly review the highlights of information gained by the team since that situation statement was composed.   5 minutes

2. Ask each team member to finish the following statement, "Based on what we have learned and done, I now think the situation is. . . ." If the team is small, responses can be shared orally. If the team is more than 6-8 people, ask each person to write their response.
5 minutes

3. a. If responses are shared orally, be alert for any changes in the situation statement. Record these changes on the flip chart. Lead the team in making any revisions to the situation statement. Record and post the revised statement.   5-10 minutes

VISTA Associates
© 1998

STEPS: 3.   b. If responses are written, ask one team member to share his response. Post the paper and ask other team members who had a similar response to read their responses, and post these responses in a cluster. Repeat this process until all responses have been collected and posted in clusters. Lead the team in making any necessary revisions to the situation statement. Record and post the revised situation statement in the group memory.   10-15 minutes

Note: Frequently the situation statement will not change and this process can be completed very quickly. However, it is important to confirm the accuracy of the situation statement before moving to the Possibilities Phase.

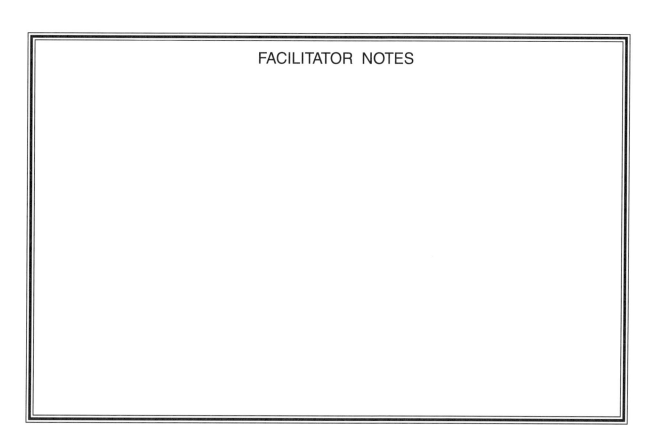

FACILITATOR NOTES

FORMING A PROPOSAL: STRAW DRAFT

The purpose of this tool is to help a task force use input from the full team to develop a draft proposal, revise the proposal, and eventually ratify the proposal as a team decision. Note: This variation was explained at the end of Chapter 5.

TIME REQUIRED:	**GROUP SIZE:**	**ROOM ARRANGEMENT:**
Varies depending on situation	4-8 member task force	Meeting space for task force

MATERIALS: Varies depending on situation

STEPS:

1. Appoint a task force of four to eight people to develop a draft proposal. Clarify that the purpose of the task force is to use the information developed by the full team during the Preparation Phase to develop a draft proposal which will address the situation being considered. The task force provides additional opportunities for full team input and continues to use the team's input to revise their original proposal until a proposal is developed that the team will support. The three rounds of gathering input and revising the proposal are known as the *Straw Draft, Wood Draft* and *Brick Draft*. With each round of input and revision, the proposal becomes more finalized and less open for major changes.

2. Schedule time for the task force to meet to develop their *Straw Draft.*

3. Schedule an opportunity for the task force to bring the *Straw Draft* back to the full team for their review and input. At this point the entire draft is open for revision. At the *Straw Draft* level all suggestions and concerns are welcome. Criticism of the *Straw Draft* should include specific suggestions for improving the proposal. The task force keeps a complete written record of all input from the full team.

4. Using the input gathered at the *Straw Draft* meeting described in Step 2, the task force makes revisions to their original proposal. This revised proposal is now known as the *Wood Draft.*

VISTA Associates
© 1998

STEPS: 5.   The task force returns the *Wood Draft* version of the proposal to the full team. During this round of input suggestions are still encouraged, but a total rewrite of the proposal is no longer acceptable. Significant modifications can still be made, but the task force can no longer be asked to totally start over. Again, a written record of all input is kept.

6.   The task force meets again to make additional revisions to their proposal using the input from the *Wood Draft* meeting. Every effort is made to respond to concerns and suggestions. The third revision of the proposal is known as the *Brick Draft*.

7.   The task force returns the *Brick Draft* to the full team for a final round of review and input. At this point, input focuses on minor refinements and adjustments. The task force is given authority to make these revisions without additional review by the full team. Following the *Brick Draft* input, the proposal is formally ratified and a decision is declared. The team can now move on to the Doing Phase.

Note: It is important that all team members understand the sequence of the *Straw/Wood/Brick Draft* process before it is used. Clarify that the process is intended to help a large team efficiently reach a decision while still honoring input from all team members. The process is also intended to honor the work of the task force and prevent endless rounds of proposals, input, new proposals, input, new proposals, etc.

If at either the *Straw* or *Wood Draft* meetings there is no significant input or requests for changes to the proposal, the team can ratify the proposal as it stands at the meeting.

FACILITATOR NOTES

ENCOURAGING DIVERGENT THINKING: BRAINSTORMING OPTIONS

The purpose of this tool is to generate multiple possibilities and options, to open up team members' thinking, to look at the situation in a variety of ways and to encourage creativity.

TIME REQUIRED:	**GROUP SIZE:**	**ROOM ARRANGEMENT:**
30 minutes or more depending on which strategy is used	Any size group	Room for participants to work in small groups

MATERIALS: For all brainstorming strategies
> **Guidelines for Brainstorming** - one per person
> Flip chart paper
> Felt tip pens

For Through the Looking Glass
> 8 1/2" x 11" sheets of paper - 10 per small group

For Pass the Cards
> Index cards - several per person

For Fill the Grid
> **Idea Grid Collection Page** - one per person

STEPS: <u>BASIC BRAINSTORMING</u>   <u>30 TO 40 MINUTES</u>

1.   Pass out the **Guidelines for Brainstorming** and review the information. Write out and post the situation question or focus of the brainstorming process. Explain that the team is going to generate as many ideas as possible that would be potential ways to deal with the situation. You might start the brainstorming by using the sentence stem, "In what ways might we. . .?"   5 minutes

2.   Divide the total team into small groups of 5-6 people. Provide each small group with flip chart pages and felt tip pens for recording ideas.   5 minutes

STEPS: 3.   Ask participants to propose ideas. Record each idea proposed on the flip chart page. Use one of the following methods to guide the sharing of ideas:
- Free-for-all: ideas are shared verbally as quickly as they occur to one of the participants.
- Round Robin: ideas are shared verbally by each participant in turn. Participants may always pass when it is their turn.
- Journaling: ideas are silently written down by each participant and then shared back to the group.   10-15 minutes

4.   Ask small groups to share their ideas with the other small groups. Like ideas are combined and a collective list is recorded on a flip chart page and posted.   10-15 minutes

VARIATIONS: FLOATING CHART   50-55 MINUTES

1.   When there are several topics about which the team needs to brainstorm, this is an effective strategy. Divide the total team into the same number of small groups as there are topics. Provide each group with a sheet of flip chart paper and a felt tip pen. Tip: If each subgroup has a different colored felt tip pen, it is easy to track where ideas were generated.   5 minutes

2.   Give each group 5 minutes to brainstorm ideas that will help explain, give examples, pose solutions or otherwise address their topic. All ideas are recorded on the subgroup's flip chart page.   5 minutes

3.   At the end of 5 minutes, each subgroup passes their chart to another subgroup. They review the recorded ideas of the previous small group and add any other ideas they may have.   5 minutes

4.   At the end of the allotted time, the groups again exchange charts. The exchanging, reviewing and adding of ideas continues until each small group receives their original chart.   15-20 minutes

5.   Ask each group to select a spokesperson who will report to the total team a summary of the information on their chart or the ideas the group thinks have the greatest potential. The charts could also be posted around the room and all participants can go on a "Wisdom Walk" reading all ideas generated.   20 minutes

VARIATIONS:

(cont'd)

<u>PASS THE CARD</u>   <u>20-40 MINUTES</u>

1.   Clarify for the team the situation that is the focus of the brainstorming. Give each participant a stack of index cards. Ask each individual to silently generate one idea and write it on one of their index cards.

                                                                                    5 minutes

2.   Ask each team member to pass their index card to the person on his right. This person reads the idea and considers whether that idea stimulates another idea for him. If so he writes down the "piggybacked" idea on another card. He may also write down a totally new idea and record it on a new index card.   5 minutes

3.   Encourage people to continue passing, "piggybacking," or generating new ideas for about ten minutes. At this time collect all cards. Cluster, post and discuss the ideas on the cards. Make a master list on the flip chart.   10-30 minutes

<u>FILL THE GRID</u>   <u>25 TO 35 MINUTES</u>

1.   Distribute an **Idea Grid Collection** page to each team member. Have each team member write down three ideas on the top row of the grid.

                                                                                    5 minutes

2.   Ask each team member to place their **Idea Grid Collection Page** in the middle of the table. When all the **Idea Grid Collection Pages** are in the middle of the table, each team member picks up a page making sure they do not take back their own **Idea Grid Collection Page**.

                                                                                    5 minutes

3.   Request that each team member add three more ideas to the **Idea Grid Collection Page** they picked up. These ideas could be completely new ideas or expansions of ideas already on the **Idea Grid Collection Page**.   5 minutes

4.   Continue exchanging pages until each **Idea Grid Collection Page** is nearly full. Encourage team members to continue to try generating new ideas, not just repeating ideas they have already recorded on another **Idea Grid Collection Page**.   5-10 minutes

5.   Ask members to take turns sharing the ideas on their last **Idea Grid Collection Page**. Other team members should cross out ideas that are repeated on their forms. Record a master list of ideas on a flip chart page that is posted where all team members can see it.

                                                                                    5-10 minutes

VARIATIONS:
(cont'd)

<u>WHAT IF. . . .</u>   <u>30 MINUTES</u>

1. When a team runs out of ideas, try this strategy. Organize a brainstorming process using the first three steps of the **Guidelines for Brainstorming**. Then use one or more of the following questions to help team members generate additional ideas:
    • What if we added new players?
    • What if we combined ideas? Combined purposes?
    • What if we made it bigger? What could we add? More time? Greater frequency? Extra value?
    • What if we made it smaller? What could we subtract? Split up? Streamline?
    • What if we rearrange it? Change the schedule? Transpose cause and effect? Change the pace?
    • What if we consider ideas that seem unacceptable today?
    • What if we substituted another process? Another place? Another approach?
    • What if money (or another resource such as time, skills or personnel) were not a restraint?   10 minutes

2. Debrief the ideas generated using any of the previously mentioned processes.   20 minutes

<u>THROUGH THE LOOKING GLASS</u>   <u>60 MINUTES</u>

1. Post the situation statement. Invite the team members to imagine that they are going to "step through the looking glass" and look at the situation from the opposite side. In other words, they are to work as if the objective of the problem is the exact opposite of reality. For example, if the issue were to develop a method for dealing with team conflict, they would take the position that they were trying to increase the difficulties experienced as a result of team conflict. After stepping through the looking glass, they brainstorm a variety of ways they can *solve* this opposite problem. In the team conflict example, they would actually think of ways to increase the team conflict. Each potential solution is written on a separate piece of paper.   10 minutes

2. Next they cluster the ideas into similar categories.   10 minutes

3. Following this, they rank the categories of ideas using a specific criteria. The criteria they use might be: most sensible to least; most exciting to least; most risky to least; aligned with goals and priorities to misaligned. As solutions are organized by category they are posted on a wall or recorded on a flip chart page.   10 minutes

VARIATIONS:
(cont'd)

<u>THROUGH THE LOOKING GLASS</u> (continued)

4. Review all of the posted information. Look for any immediate aha's. Share and record if there are any.   5 minutes

5. Now invite team members to step back through the looking glass. Ask them to assume the real focus of the problem. Using the example given in Step 1, you would ask them to focus on finding a process for productively resolving team conflict.   5 minutes

6. Lead a discussion about potential solutions.
    - Do any of the "through the looking glass" solutions have potential as real solutions?
    - Could any of the "through the looking glass" solutions be reversed and provide the basis for an appropriate solution to the actual problem?
    - How would we rank order the reversed ideas using the criteria applied in Step 3?

    Record all of the ideas generated by the above process and use them in the decision making process.   20 minutes

---

FACILITATOR NOTES

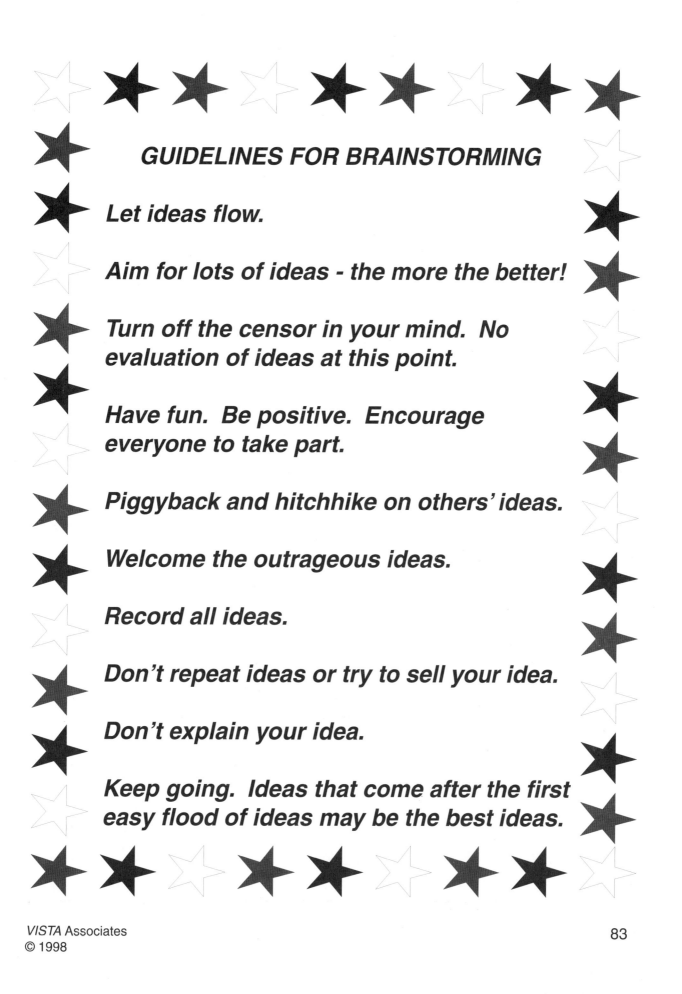

GUIDELINES FOR BRAINSTORMING

Let ideas flow.

Aim for lots of ideas - the more the better!

Turn off the censor in your mind. No evaluation of ideas at this point.

Have fun. Be positive. Encourage everyone to take part.

Piggyback and hitchhike on others' ideas.

Welcome the outrageous ideas.

Record all ideas.

Don't repeat ideas or try to sell your idea.

Don't explain your idea.

Keep going. Ideas that come after the first easy flood of ideas may be the best ideas.

IDEA GRID COLLECTION PAGE

PROMOTING DIALOGUE:
COMPASS QUESTIONS

POSSIBILITIES

The purpose of this tool is to provide direction for teams as they dialogue about various options generated during brainstorming.

TIME REQUIRED:	**GROUP SIZE:**	**ROOM ARRANGEMENT:**
25 minutes or more depending on the number of options being explored	Any size	Team members need to be able to see and hear each other and easily see any posted flip chart pages.

MATERIALS: Flip chart
Felt tip pens
Overhead projector
Blank transparency
Vis-a-vis pens
Compass Questions - written on flip chart page and posted or projected as a transparency

STEPS:

1. On flip chart pages record all the options brainstormed in Step 4 of the Possibilities Phase described on page 53. Post them so they are visible to all team members. Also, write the **Compass Questions** on a flip chart page or make a transparency of the questions you will be using.   Prior to the start of the meeting

2. Facilitate team members in reviewing the **Compass Questions**. If time is limited, team members should select two or three questions to use as the basis of their dialogue.   5 minutes

3. Begin with the first selected Compass Question and lead the team in a dialogue about the implication of the answers to that question as they scan the posted options. Record team member comments on a flip chart page.   10 minutes

STEPS: 4. Repeat Step 3 for each remaining Compass Question. Record team member comments on the flip chart. This written record may be helpful as the team continues to work through the consensus process.

10 minutes per Compass Question

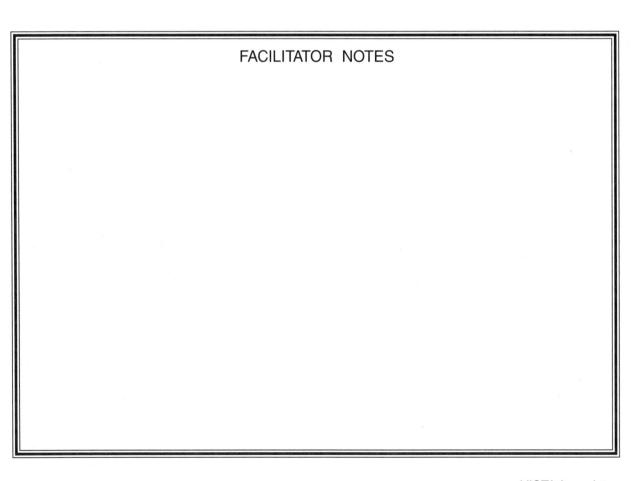

FACILITATOR NOTES

COMPASS
QUESTIONS

Which options draw your energy and attention? Why?

Which options make you uncomfortable? Why?

Which options would be a real stretch? Why?

Which options surprise you? Why?

Which options could be combined into one?

Which options exclude each other?

Which options need clarification?

Do you see a pattern across the options?

SIGNALING MY OPINION:
FIST TO FIVE

The purpose of this tool is to probe for the opinion of individual team members regarding an option under consideration.

TIME REQUIRED:

40 minutes

GROUP SIZE:

Any size group

ROOM ARRANGEMENT:

Any room arrangement

MATERIALS: Flip Chart
Marking pens
Fist to Five transparency

STEPS: 1.   Show the **Fist to Five** transparency and explain the three ways team members can express individual opinions. State the option being considered. Confirm that everyone has the same understanding of the option. Clarify that this is a *probe*.   5 minutes

2.   Team members express their opinion of the option under consideration by holding up 5 fingers, 3 fingers or a fist. Tabulate the total of each and record the information on the flip chart.   5 minutes

3.   Choose one of the following variations depending on the results of Step 2.

VARIATION A: If the majority of the hands showed all five fingers you would:

• Ask those with a fist to say why it is not possible to accept the option. Record these reasons on the flip chart.   5 minutes

• Ask those with 3 fingers showing to express their concerns. Record these concerns on the flip chart.   5 minutes

• Ask some of those with 5 fingers showing to speak for the option.   5 minutes

VISTA Associates
© 1998

VARIATION A:
(cont'd)

• Engage the team in a discussion about the option to give the team members who expressed a 3 finger or fist opinion the opportunity to influence those team members who had expressed 5 fingers of support. 15 minutes

VARIATION B:

If the majority of the hands show three fingers or a fist:

• Ask the team members with 5 fingers to say why they support the decision. Record this information on the flip chart. 5 minutes

• Ask some of those with 3 fingers to share their reasons and record them on the flip chart. 5 minutes

• Ask some of those with a fist to share their reasons and record them on the flip chart. 5 minutes

• Conduct a team discussion to give the team members with a support of 5 fingers the opportunity to influence those who did not support the option. Try to problem solve any of the concerns raised. 15 minutes

If there is no clear majority in any of the three opinion groups:

VARIATION C:

• Explain that you will gather a sample of reasons for the three different levels of opinion. Call on three to five of those with fists, then those signaling three fingers and finally with 5 fingers showing. Record all the comments. 15 minutes

• Facilitate a team discussion giving every opinion group the opportunity to influence the others. Try to address concerns and reasons for nonsupport if possible. 15 minutes

Note: After a team discussion you may want to call for a second Fist to Five vote. As with all strategies, you should be careful not to over use this method of probing.

FACILITATOR NOTES

FIST TO FIVE

FIVE FINGERS:
<u>**Total agreement**</u>
This is the best solution and I give complete support.

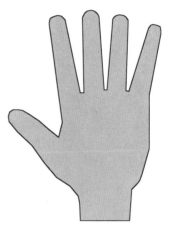

THREE FINGERS:
<u>**Willing to support**</u>
I could live with this, but I have a concern.

FIST:
<u>**Will not support**</u>
I have serious concerns and prefer we not consider this option.

DISPLAYING PREFERENCES:
MULTI -VOTING

The purpose of this tool is to reduce a long list of options to a list of preferred options.

TIME REQUIRED:	GROUP SIZE:	ROOM ARRANGEMENT:
40 minutes or more depending on number of rounds	Any size group	A room with adequate wall space to display charts with the options

MATERIALS: List of options under consideration on flip chart paper
Masking tape
Felt tip pens
Sticky dots - several per participant

STEPS:

1. Prepare a list of options currently being considered by the team on flip chart pages and post these pages so all team members can easily read the list.   Prior to the start of the meeting

2. Ask each person to read the list of options. Check to see if there are any questions.   5 minutes

3. Clarify that this activity is a *probe*. Direct each participant to select the options he prefers by placing a sticky dot by those options. Each participant is allowed a number of votes (sticky dots) equal to one-third the total number of options on the list. If there are 15 items on the list, each person identifies 5 items. They may not put more than one dot on a single option. When the dotting is complete, remove items from the list that did not receive any votes.   5 minutes

4. Discuss options that were voted for by less than 25% of the participants. If everyone agrees to remove an item, do so. However, if after discussion the person(s) who originally voted for the option still thinks it is very important, it is left on the list for another vote. Only the members who voted for an option can remove it from the list.
                                                                                15 minutes

STEPS: 5.   Repeat Steps 2 through 4 with the remaining options, voting and reducing the list until only a few options (generally a maximum of three to five) remain. Record these in the group memory.

15 minutes

Note: If it is helpful to identify the choices of various segments within the organization, different colored dots can be given to different groups. For example, Marketing can use blue dots while Research and Development can use yellow dots.

FACILITATOR NOTES

SETTING THE STANDARDS: CRITERIA SORT

The purpose of this tool is to establish criteria to use in evaluating preferred options.

PROBING

TIME REQUIRED:	**GROUP SIZE:**	**ROOM ARRANGEMENT:**
1 hour, 55 minutes to 2 hours, 10 minutes	Any size group	Tables for groups of 4-6 people

MATERIALS:
8 1/2" x 11" paper - several sheets per small group
Felt tip pens - one per small group
Flip chart
Overhead projector, screen, and vis-a-vis pens
Blank transparencies
Sticky dots - 9 per person (3 each of 3 different colors)
Defining Criteria transparency
Categories of Criteria transparency
Criteria Weight transparency

STEPS:

1. Facilitate a team dialogue about criteria. Begin by showing the **Defining Criteria** transparency and engage the team in a conversation about this definition:

    A criteria is a judgement or rule used for evaluating something.   5 minutes

2. Explain the need for clear criteria against which the options for a decision can be evaluated. Remind them that they eliminated some options in Step 6 of the Probing Phase on page 54. Clarify that this criteria will be applied to the remaining options.   5 minutes

3. Show the **Categories of Criteria** transparency. Explain that there are groups or categories of criteria the team should keep in mind when evaluating options. These categories include:
    Options that can be implemented with reasonable:
    - time
    - money
    - staffing
    - effort
    - learning and training
    Options that match the core beliefs and vision of the team.
                            10 minutes

STEPS: 4.   Briefly review the situation statement. Ask the team to determine which criteria from the **Categories of Criteria** transparency apply to this situation. List those categories that do apply on the flip chart. Next ask the team to determine if any unique category of criteria should be added to help them effectively evaluate options. Add any additional criteria categories to the flip chart list.   10 minutes

5.   Organize the team into small groups of 4 to 6 people and request that each small group brainstorm specific criteria for evaluating the remaining options, keeping in mind the categories of criteria listed on the flip chart. They should record each potential criteria on a separate sheet of paper using a felt tip pen. This step needs to be customized for various size groups.
   a. In teams of ten or less, ask people to work in pairs to generate the potential criteria.
   b. In teams of 11 to 30 organize them into groups of 4 to 6 people and ask them to generate their lists of criteria.
   c. In teams with more than 30 members, appoint a task force of team members. This task force completes the remaining steps in this tool and reports the list of specific criteria to the full team.   30 minutes

6.   Ask one small group to post one of the criteria they have recorded. Invite all the other groups to purge this one from their collection of criteria if they had also written it. Next, ask another group to post one of their suggested criteria and again the other groups purge it. Repeat this post and purge process until all criteria are posted and there are no duplicates. Inform them they can add a new potential criteria at any time during this post and purge step.   15-30 minutes

7.   Show the **Criteria Weight** transparency and teach or review the three weights of criteria:
   Critical: An option must match this criteria if we are to reach our goal.
   Important: An option should match this criteria if at all possible.
   Would Be Nice: An option might meet this criteria, but it is not essential.   5 minutes

8.   Ask people to gather their 9 sticky dots. Designate one of the three colors for *critical* and ask everyone to label these three with the word *critical*. Check that everyone is using the correct color. Designate a different color for *important* and ask them to write the word *important* on these three dots. Direct them to label the last three dots with the words *would be nice*.   5 minutes

STEPS: 9.   Review the posted potential criteria generated by the team in Step 6. Inform the team members that they are now going to prioritize their potential criteria by using the weights learned in Step 7. Request that everyone gather their three *critical* dots (remind them of the color) and place them on the three criteria they think are critical for the successful accomplishment of the decision goal. They are to place one dot per criteria and they may not double dot. They do not have to use all three of their dots. Tabulate the results and list the *critical* criteria (the two or three criteria with the most dots) on the flip chart. Label this list of criteria as "critical."   10 minutes

10.   Ask people to place their *important* dots (remind them of the color) on the criteria they think should be met if at all possible. Again, they place one dot per criteria and do not double dot. Make it clear that they may dot any of the items that had been previously dotted as *critical* but were not one of the top two or three. Tabulate the results and add the *important* criteria to the flip chart list. Label this list of criteria as "important."   10 minutes

11.   Request that people take their *would be nice* dots and place them on the criteria they think are helpful, but not essential to reaching the goal for the decision. Again, they can place them on any criteria except those already listed as *critical* or *important*, placing one dot per criteria and not double dotting. Tabulate the results and create a list of "would be nice" criteria (the two or three items with the most dots) on the flip chart. Confirm the complete list of chosen criteria and the weight of each criteria item.   10 minutes

---

FACILITATOR NOTES

Defining Criteria

A criteria is a judgement or rule used for evaluating something.

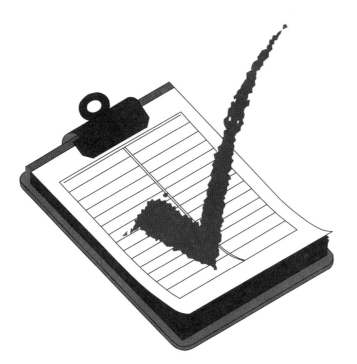

Categories
of Criteria

Options requiring reasonable:
- **time**
- **money**
- **staffing**
- **effort**
- **learning and training**

Options matching core beliefs and vision of the team

Criteria Weight

<u>Critical</u>: An option must match this criteria if we are to reach our goal.

<u>Important</u>: An option should match this criteria if at all possible.

<u>Would Be Nice</u>: An option might meet this criteria, but it is not essential.

ANALYZING OPTIONS: OPTION/CRITERIA MATCH

PROBING

The purpose of this tool is to analyze high priority options against set criteria.

TIME REQUIRED:	GROUP SIZE:	ROOM ARRANGEMENT:
1 hour 40 minutes to 2 hours	Any size group	Any room arrangement

MATERIALS: **Analyzing Options: Option/Criteria Match** - one worksheet per person
Flip chart
Felt tip pens

STEPS:

1. Review the criteria named in the tool, Setting the Standards: Criteria Sort. Be sure that each criteria is clearly stated and understood by those who will do the analysis.   15 minutes

2. Ask each team member to list the criteria on the *Criteria* column of his matrix.   5 minutes

3. Review the weight assigned each criteria in Setting the Standards: Criteria Sort. Remind team members of the following:
   - 3 = critical, option must meet the criteria*
   - 2 = important, option will meet the criteria if at all possible
   - 1 = would be nice, option might meet criteria but it is not essential.

   *Emphasize that a weight of three on a criteria is so strong that if an option does not match a level three criteria, the option is dropped from further consideration. It is essentially vetoed.

   Ask each team member to record the criteria weight for each criteria on the analysis chart in the *Criteria Weight* column.   10 minutes

4. List the previously identified options across the top of the chart under *Options*.   5 minutes

STEPS:

5. Individually analyze the first option against the first criteria using the following scale:

        5 = option matches the criteria

        3 = option somewhat matches the criteria

        1 = option does not match the criteria   **15 minutes**

6, Record this number for the criteria in the *Criteria Match* column on the analysis chart.   **5 minutes**

7. Multiply the criteria weight times the criteria match. Record the total for each criteria in the *Criteria Total* column on the analysis chart.   **5 minutes**

8. Repeat steps 5, 6 and 7 for all remaining options.   **20-40 minutes**

9. Add the *Criteria Total* column for the first option and record the total on the *Total* line at the bottom of the analysis chart. Repeat for the remaining options.   **5 minutes**

10. Identify the option with the <u>highest</u> total and name it as the strongest match to the criteria.   **5 minutes**

11. Average individual scores to obtain an analysis total for the entire team.   **10 minutes**

Note: It may be necessary to expand the grid if there are more than four criteria. To use time efficiently, team members can complete their individual **Analyzing Options: Option Criteria Match** worksheet outside the meeting and turn in their completed sheets to the facilitator for averaging. The results can be shared with the full team at the next meeting.

FACILITATOR NOTES

ANALYZING OPTIONS: OPTION/CRITERIA MATCH

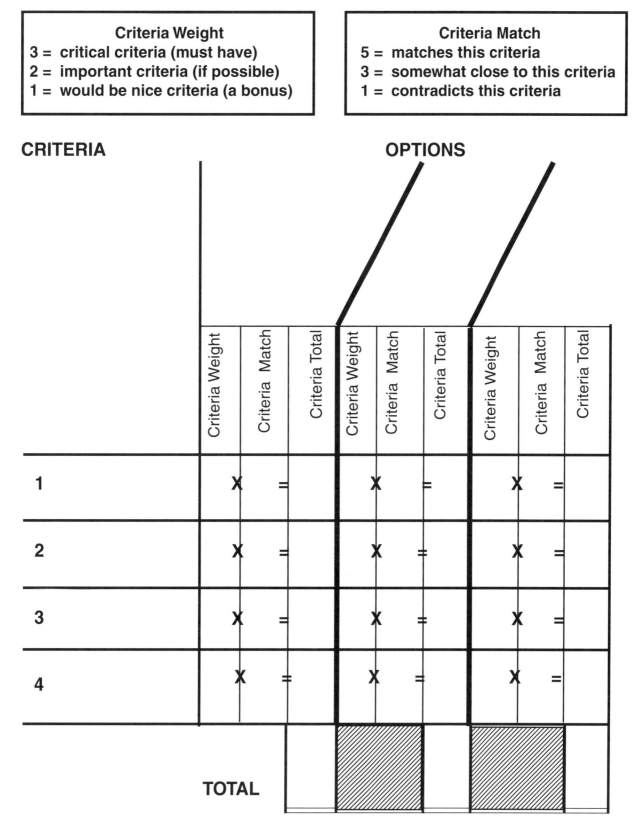

Criteria Weight
3 = critical criteria (must have)
2 = important criteria (if possible)
1 = would be nice criteria (a bonus)

Criteria Match
5 = matches this criteria
3 = somewhat close to this criteria
1 = contradicts this criteria

CRITERIA

OPTIONS

	Criteria Weight	Criteria Match	Criteria Total	Criteria Weight	Criteria Match	Criteria Total	Criteria Weight	Criteria Match	Criteria Total
1	X	=		X	=		X	=	
2	X	=		X	=		X	=	
3	X	=		X	=		X	=	
4	X	=		X	=		X	=	
TOTAL									

DISPLAYING OUR OPINIONS:
LEVELS OF YES AND NO

PROBING

The purpose of this tool is to provide a visual display of the position held by all team members on an option being considered by the team, inventory concerns, and support addressing these concerns.

TIME REQUIRED:

1 hour 10 minutes to
1 hour 30 minutes

GROUP SIZE:

Any size group

ROOM ARRANGEMENT:

Participants at tables with clear view of flip chart

MATERIALS:
Flip chart
Felt tip markers
3 inch square post notes - two per team member

STEPS:

1. Clarify the option that the team is considering. Write the option on the top of a flip chart page. Ask team members to pair up and share their understanding of the option with one another checking to see if all team members can paraphrase the option being considered. Emphasize that this is a *probe*.   5 minutes

2. Facilitate a dialogue and discussion about the option. During the dialogue, everyone suspends their judgments and opinions and is willing to be influenced by other people. Members of the team paraphrase frequently, ask clarifying questions and take care to listen both accurately and empathetically. During the discussion, group members state their opinions and argue their point.   10 minutes

3. After the dialogue and discussion, reclarify the option. Read the statement from Step 1 and ask if everyone still agrees that this really is the option being considered. If the answer is yes, the group proceeds. If the answer is no, repeat the process used in Step 1.
                                                                                     5 minutes

4. When the group agrees that the option statement is accurate, replicate the chart below on the flip chart page underneath the option statement.

Levels of No									Levels of Yes
1	2	3	4	5	6	7	8	9	10

STEPS: 4.   Walk the group through the levels of *no* and *yes* explaining the
   (cont'd)   following:

          1....absolutely not
          2....strongly no
          3....no
          4....somewhat opposed
          5....mildly opposed
          6....mildly in favor
          7....somewhat in favor
          8....yes
          9....strongly yes
          10....absolutely yes   5 minutes

5.   Ask team members to think about the situation and choose the number that best represents their current opinions about the option. Request that each person record his number on one of the 3 inch square post notes provided. Next, ask everyone to write a brief statement of rationale giving the reason for his rating on the post note underneath the numberon the post note. Signing names on the post note is helpful but optional.   5 minutes

7.   Ask participants to place the post notes on the flip chart in a column under the number that matches the rating on his post note. The resulting vertical bar graph provides a visual display of opinions held by the team.   5 minutes

8.   Read the statements of rationale from all of the post notes. Ask people to listen analytically, looking for categories of rationale as well as similarities and differences among the categories.   5-10 minutes

9.   Focus the team on the rationale statements that express a concern. Be sure to examine concerns from both the *No* and *Yes* sides of the chart. It is helpful to begin with the concerns that have been mentioned most frequently.   5 minutes

10.   Invite people to speak for the *No* side of the option. Others can ask questions of those who choose to speak. Then ask people to speak for the *Yes* side of the issue. Again, others can ask questions of those who speak. Remind all team members to stay open to the influence of others.   15 - 30 minutes

STEPS: 11. Do a second round by repeating Steps 6 and 7. Ask the team to evaluate the Levels of Yes and No chart to determine if *most* has been reached on either side. If *most* has been reached on the *No* side, this option is rejected and the team must move on to the next option. If *most* has been reached on the *Yes* side, the team will move to the Declaring Phase. Regardless of the results, label the flip chart page "Probe."   10 minutes

Note: When the group is larger than 30 people, divide the team into small groups of 4-6 people for discussion and problem solving. Provide some time for small groups to report back to the entire team.

VARIATION: Displaying Our Opinions: Levels of Yes and No can also be used in the Declaring Phase to state the final decision of the team. In that case, Repeat Step 6. This time each team member signs his name to his post note. Declare that a decision has been made. Date and label the flip chart page as "Decision Declared."

FACILITATOR NOTES

LABELING THE LEVELS: CUSTOMIZING SUPPORT

DECLARING

The purpose of this tool is to stipulate the level of support given by each individual on the team for the implementation of the decision.

TIME REQUIRED:

1 hour 15 minutes

GROUP SIZE:

Any size group

ROOM ARRANGEMENT:

Any room arrangement

MATERIALS: **Customizing Support** worksheet - one per participant
Flip chart
Felt tip pens

STEPS: 1. Communicate to the team that *most* has been or is close to being reached. Point out that it is time to ask team members to overtly indicate what is required at each level of support. Individuals need to indicate what they are willing to do toward the implementation of the decision. Distribute the **Customizing Support** worksheets.

15 minutes

2. Assist the team members in deciding what the levels of support will look like as they collaborate for a successful implementation of the decision. Help them answer the following questions:

What will it look like if people are willing to give <u>minimal support</u> to this decision?

What is/are the critical thing(s) that is/are required of team members to insure successful implementation of this decision?

What will it look like if people are willing to give <u>moderate support</u> to this decision?

What would team members need to say or do to indicate they were willing to make a positive effort to support the implementation of the decision?

What will it look like if people are willing to give <u>proactive support</u> to this decision?

What would team members need to be willing to do to plan the implementation of the decision? What task forces, committees will be necessary for the implementation of the decision?

STEPS: 2.   What will it look like if people are willing to give <u>maximum support</u> to
(cont'd)   the implementation of the decision?

> What will team members do to assume a leadership role in the implementation of the decision? What leadership role(s) is/are essential to the implementation of the decision?

Encourage the team to specify the behaviors that would be expected at each of the four levels of support. Make it clear that a decision cannot be implemented if the behaviors necessary for implementing the decision are not articulated. If the group is larger than twelve people, form quartets and facilitate each foursome in specifying the behaviors. Synthesize the information into a list that represents the whole team.   45 minutes

   3.   Record the agreed upon behaviors for each level of support in the group memory.   15 minutes

VARIATION: Record each of the four levels of support on four different flip chart pages. Include the specific behaviors articulated by the team for each of the four levels. Post these pages, starting with the minimal page and ending with the maximum page. Then ask team members to sign the chart that describes the level of support they are willing to give to the implementation of the decision.

FACILITATOR NOTES

CUSTOMIZING SUPPORT

Decision

MINIMAL SUPPORT Do what is critical.	MODERATE SUPPORT Make a positive effort.	PROACTIVE SUPPORT Help it happen.	MAXIMUM SUPPORT Lead the effort.
At this level of support a team member is expected to do only those things that are critical to the successful implementation of the decision.	At this level of support a team member is expected to go beyond the bare essentials by making an authentic contribution to the successful implementation of the decision.	At this level of support a team member is expected to advocate the success of the decision by helping plan the implementation as well as assisting in the monitoring and working of the plan.	At this level of support a team member is expected to support colleagues and to provide leadership in planning, implementing and evaluating the decision.
Minimal support includes:	Moderate support includes:	Proactive support includes:	Maximum support includes:
•	•	•	•
•	•	•	•
•	•	•	•
•	•	•	•

DECLARING OUR AGREEMENT AND CONTRIBUTION: COMMITMENT CONTINUUM

The purpose of this tool is to display the distribution of agreement with the option and level of contribution people are willing to give to the implementation of the decision.

TIME REQUIRED:

1 hour 15 minutes

GROUP SIZE:

Any size group

ROOM ARRANGEMENT:

Any room arrangement

MATERIALS: Two sticky dots per participant
Commitment Continuum chart

STEPS:

1. Draw the **Commitment Continuum** chart on a flip chart page.

   Prior to the meeting

2. Record the option being considered on the flip chart or on a transparency. Facilitate a dialogue to ensure that all team members have a common understanding of the option.   5 minutes

3. Specify that this is a *declare* activity. Remind the team that *most* has been reached, i.e., the necessary percentage of team members has agreed to an option during a previous probe. As a team they will be confirming a decision that will require action for the implementation.

   5 minutes

4. Clarify the meaning of the levels of yes and no. Explain that: strong disagreement indicates a person thinks the option is a serious mistake.

   1...meaning absolutely not
   2...strongly no

   Disagreement indicates a person has some concerns about the option.

   3...no
   4...somewhat opposed
   5...mildly opposed

   Agreement indicates a person thinks the option is workable.

   6...mildly in favor
   7...somewhat in favor

   Strong agreement indicates a person thinks this option is the best.

   8...yes
   9...strongly yes
   10...absolutely yes   5 minutes

STEPS: 5.   Give each team member two sticky dots and ask them to place one dot on the number that matches their current level of agreement or disagreement regarding the option.   10 minutes

6.   Compute and announce the results indicated by the dots. Again confirm that *most* has been reached.   5 minutes

7.   Remind people that everyone will participate in mutual problem solving as the decision is implemented. Then review the meaning of the levels of support. Explain that:

Minimal Support means, "I'll do the bare essentials."
Moderate Support means, "I will give it a positive effort."
Proactive Support means, "I will be on the committee, collect data, attend meetings."
Maximum Support means, "I will chair a committee."
15 minutes

8.   Invite participants to place their second dot on the number that represents their willingness to support the decision, i.e., to contribute to the successful implementation of the decision.   15 minutes

9.   Debrief the results indicated by the dots. Note whether or not there are sufficient dots in the maximum and proactive sections on the support side of the continuum to ensure implementation. If not, the team needs to problem solve this situation. It is essential that some team members be willing to lead the implementation and some willing to work proactively toward the successful implementation. If this is not the case, the decision is likely to fail. Once there is a sufficient number of dots in these two categories, the decision is officially declared and the team moves to developing the action plan for the implementation of the decision. Note this in the group memory.
15 minutes

FACILITATOR NOTES

COMMITMENT CONTINUUM

Level of Yes/No		Level of Contribution
Strong Agreement I think this is our best option.	10 9 8	**Maximum Support** I will lead/facilitate the planning, implementation and evaluation.
Agreement I think this is a workable option.	7 6	**Proactive Support** I'll help plan and carry out the comprehensive implementation.
Disagreement I have some concerns.	5 4 3	**Moderate Support** As an individual, I will look for things I can do to support implementation.
Strong Disagreement I think this is a mistake.	2 1	**Minimal Support** As an individual, I'll do what is necessary to support the decision.

DECLARING OUR UNITY: STEPPING UP TO SUPPORT

The purpose of this tool is to physically display and confirm *gifting* support for the implementation of the decision by all team members.

TIME REQUIRED:

45 to 50 minutes

GROUP SIZE:

Any size group

ROOM ARRANGEMENT:

A room with enough space so people can line up on either side of the room

MATERIALS:

Questions transparency
Flip chart
Felt tip pens
Overhead projector and screen
Blank transparencies
Vis-a-vis pens

STEPS:

1. Write the option that has been declared as the decision on the flip chart or on a blank transparency. Invite people to form pairs or trios and paraphrase the decision to confirm they understand the decision.
   5 minutes

2. Request that people consider their opinion of the decision that has been declared. Ask them to move to the left side of room if they disagree with the decision or move to the right side if they agree with the decision.
   5 minutes

3. Review the concept of *Gifting* Support (see Chapter 3, pages 27-30). Ask people to pair up and share their individual understanding of the concept. Emphasize that *gifting* support is much easier for those on the agree side of the room. These are the team members who make up the *most* for this decision. It is more difficult for those in the *few*, those on the disagree side of the room.
   10 minutes

4. Show the **Questions** transparency and ask each person to briefly reflect on his answers to the questions. Request that the people on the agree side of the room walk to the center to acknowledge their support. Briefly gather a few comments explaining why they support the decision.
   10 minutes

STEPS: 5. Then ask those on the disagree side of the room, "Can you *gift* support to the implementation of this decision?" If they can answer "yes," they are to move one at a time to the center of the room, stating as they walk what made it possible for them to *gift* their support.

10-15 minutes

6. As a facilitator acknowledge appreciation to the *few* for their *gifting* of support for the successful implementation of the decision. Make clear that the support of all team members is necessary if the decision is to be successfully implemented.

5 minutes

Note: If a team member refuses to *gift* try one of these options:

OPTIONS: A. Ask: " (Person's name), what would be necessary for you to *gift* your support?"

B. "Person's name, let me ask you the four *gifting* questions." Place the **Questions** transparency on the overhead and ask them the questions in order. After the answers have been stated, remind the team members that if the questions have been answered "Yes," by the very definition of consensus, the team members in the *few* are to *gift* their support.

C. Explain the minimal support expectations generated in the tool, Labeling the Levels: Customizing Support on page 105. Then ask if the person is willing to *gift* that level of support. If the person answers "yes," invite him to the center of the room. If no, set up a meeting between you, the person refusing to *gift* support, the person's supervisor and a colleague of that person's choice. In this meeting try to help the person see that *gifting* is his responsibility.

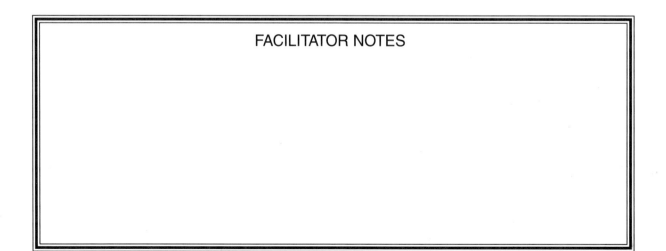

FACILITATOR NOTES

Have I clearly stated my position during our previous discussions?

Have I been heard and understood?

Have my concerns been addressed?

Do I understand the option declared as the decision?

DEVELOPING THE DETAILS:
AN ACTION PLAN

DOING

The purpose of this tool is to develop a plan that clearly states who is responsible for what in implementing the decision, as well as the timelines and criteria for evaluating the various actions in the implementation process.

TIME REQUIRED:

1 hour 15 minutes plus 10 to 25 minutes per action step

GROUP SIZE:

Any group size

ROOM ARRANGEMENT:

Any room arrangement

MATERIALS:

3 inch square post notes
Action Plan Form
Flip chart
Felt tip pens

STEPS:

1. Prior to the meeting, prepare an **Action Plan Form** on a flip chart page in the group memory.   Prior to the meeting

2. State the decision that is the focus of the action plan. Record it on the top of the **Action Plan Form**.   5 minutes

3. Facilitate a discussion of the various actions that must be done to insure the successful implementation of the decision. Write each action on a separate post note.   20 minutes

4. Assist the team members in arranging the action steps on the **Action Plan Form** in sequential order in the *What* column. Sometimes it is helpful to start with the action step that will be completed last and work backwards to the first step.   20 minutes

5. When all the action steps have been posted, begin with the first step and identify the person who will take leadership responsibility for this action step and record his name in the *Who* section. Mark this name with an asterisk to indicate leadership responsibilities. If a person assigned leadership responsibility is not in attendance, the action plan should indicate who will contact that person to explain the assignment and to seek his acceptance of the responsibility.   5 minutes

STEPS: 6. Clarify who should be involved in this action step and record these name(s) in the who section on the **Action Plan Form**.   5 minutes

7. Ask the person with leadership responsibility to state when the action step will be started and when it will be completed. If necessary, input and recommendations can be made by other team members. When the dates are decided, they are recorded in the *When* section on the **Action Plan Form**. 5 minutes

8. Ask what resources will be needed and record these in the *Resource* section on the **Action Plan Form**.   5 minutes

9. Facilitate the team deciding how they will know that the action step has been successfully completed and write that on the *Evaluation Data* section on the **Action Plan Form**.   5 minutes

10. Repeat Steps 5 through 9 with each action step on the plan, filling in each column on the action plan form. The time will vary depending on the number and complexity of the steps.   10 to 25 minutes per action

11. step

When the **Action Plan** is complete, an Implementation Chairperson should be appointed. It is the responsibility of this person to monitor the progress of the implementation and troubleshoot any blocks that occur.   5 minutes

Note: For teams of more than 30 people it is advisable to form a representative task force to create the action plan.

FACILITATOR NOTES

ACTION PLAN FORM

Decision _____

WHAT	WHO Responsible	WHEN Start / End	RESOURCES	EVALUATION DATA

TRACKING OUR PROGRESS: A WALL CHART DISPLAY

DOING

The purpose of this tool is to provide a public display of progress in implementing the decision as well as an efficient means to share concerns and solutions to concerns.

TIME REQUIRED:

20 minutes of full team time

GROUP SIZE:

Any group size

ROOM ARRANGEMENT:

Blank space on a wall in a central location that is convenient for all team members

MATERIALS: Wall chart replica of the action plan
Implementation Update Chart
Flip chart
Felt tip pens

STEPS:

1. Prepare a large wall size replica of the action plan prepared in Step 13 of the Doing Phase described on page 57. Also prepare an **Implementation Update Chart**.   Prior to the meeting

2. Explain the purpose and location of the wall chart replica to the full team. Make it clear that there will be a chart for each decision that has an action plan to support its implementation.   2 minutes

3. Inform the team that when people have completed items on the action plan for which they are responsible they will highlight that item on the wall chart. Note that this will provide an interesting, ongoing visual display of implementation progress. Also explain that the implementation chair appointed in the tool, Developing the Details: An Action Plan, will monitor the chart and make necessary inquiries and reminders should deadlines not be met.   3 minutes

4. Distribute the samples of the **Implementation Update Chart** and explain how it will be used. Record a sample concern about the implementation of the decision in the *Concerns* column of the sample chart. Date the entry and sign your name.   10 minutes

STEPS: 5.   Ask team members to volunteer some suggestions how they might help with that concern. Invite one of them to write his or her suggestion in the *Solutions and Suggestions* column with the date and the person's signature. Explain that the **Implementation Update Chart** provides a means for ongoing problem solving and team collaboration. Note that the implementation chair will monitor this chart and if he thinks one of the concerns should be discussed by the full team, he will place that item on the agenda for an upcoming meeting.

10 minutes

6.   Explain that the *Important Information* column will be used by the committee and individuals to share information that is critical to the effective implementation of the decision. Confirm that periodic summaries of the **Implementation Update Charts** will be shared at full team meetings.   10 minutes

VARIATION: The wall chart replica and **Implementation Update Chart** can be done electronically and the communication shared via the team's computer network. Some teams like to use both the electronic and the paper versions as a means of monitoring progress and sharing critical information.

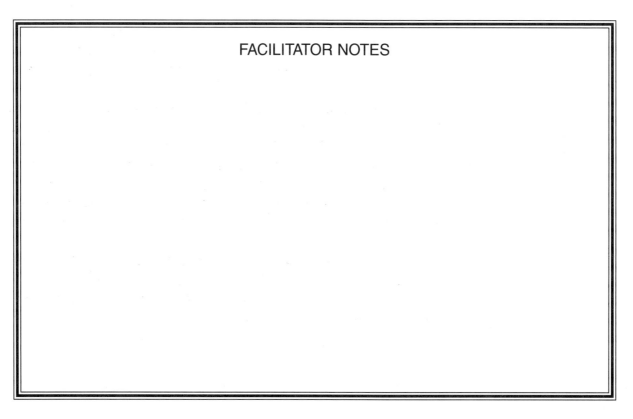

FACILITATOR NOTES

IMPLEMENTATION UPDATE CHART

Decision

Concerns, Questions, Requests for Help	Solutions, Suggestions, Offers of Help	Important Information

Be sure to sign and date your entries on this chart. Thanks!

EVALUATING THE RESULTS: QUESTIONS AND ANSWERS

DOING

TOOL

The purpose of this tool is to guide team dialogue about the successes and failures that have occurred during the implementation of the decision.

TIME REQUIRED:	**GROUP SIZE:**	**ROOM ARRANGEMENT:**
15 to 90 minutes	Any size group	Any room arrangement

MATERIALS:
Flip chart
Felt tip pens
Overhead projector, screen and vis-a-vis pens
Blank transparencies

STEPS:

1. Examine the following list of questions and choose those appropriate for guiding your team in a dialogue about the quality of the results generated by the implementation of the decision.

    Prior to the meeting

    Questions:
    When we compare the baseline data and benchmark data, did we get the increase(s) or decrease(s) we targeted?
    > If the answer is yes, plan how to sustain this result. If the answer is no, analyze why and plan next steps to meet that target for improvement.

    Were there unexpected surprise benefits? What were they?

    Were there unexpected surprise losses? What were they?

    As a result of this implementation are we closer to realizing our vision?

    As a result of this implementation are we achieving any of our major goals or priorities?

    What have we learned about making decisions as a team?

    What have we learned about this situation in particular?

    What have we learned about ourselves as a team?

STEPS: 2. Show the first question you selected. Ask people to think about their response. Invite them to pair up with one teammate and compare their thoughts. 5 minutes

3. Engage in a full team dialogue; sharing, recording and comparing responses across the team. 10 minutes

4. Repeat Steps 2 and 3 with the other questions you have chosen. It is advisable to limit the dialogue to six or fewer questions.

Note: It is helpful to develop additional, customized questions that fit the culture of your team and the nature of individual decisions. We suggest you record these questions in the *Facilitator Notes* section below.

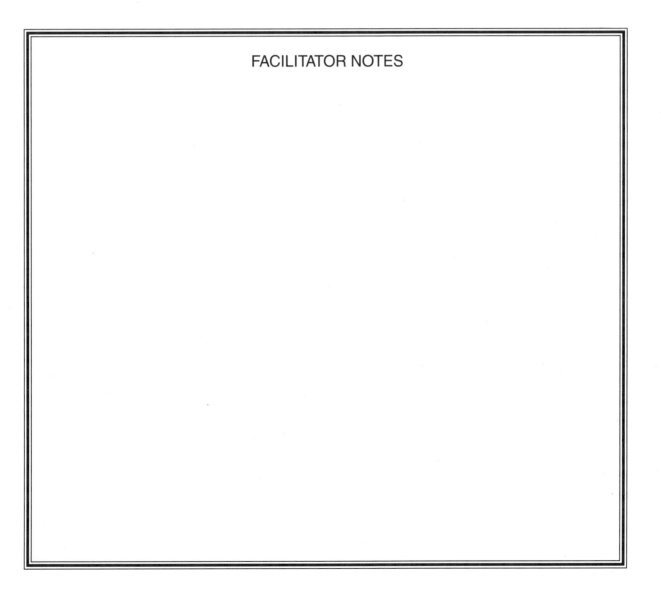

FACILITATOR NOTES

WEAVING A WEB OF CELEBRATION: CONSIDERING THE RESULTS

The purpose of this tool is to formally celebrate the achievements of the team.

TIME REQUIRED:

20 minutes plus 2 minutes per person

GROUP SIZE:

5 to 60

ROOM ARRANGEMENT:

A chair for each person arranged in a circle

MATERIALS:

Overhead projector, screen
Vis-a-vis pens
Blank transparencies
Flip chart
Felt tip pens
Ball of brightly colored yarn

STEPS:

1. Create one or two sentence stems you want to use to guide the celebration. For example, "The best result from our work is...." Record the stem on a blank transparency.   Prior to the meeting

2. At the meeting briefly review the original situation and the resulting decision. Summarize the information from the evaluation completed in the tool, Evaluating Results: Questions and Answers.   5 minutes

3. Show the ball of yarn to the team and explain that each participant will have a chance to hold the ball of yarn. While they are holding it, they are to respond to the sentence stem on the screen. 5 minutes

4. Model by holding the ball of yarn and sharing your response. Record your comment on the flip chart.   2 minutes

5. Keep the end of the ball of yarn and toss it to another person. Invite this person to share his response. Record this response. Ask him to take hold of the yarn at the place it is coming from the ball while he unwinds a portion of yarn several yards long. While maintaining his original hold, he tosses the yarn to another team member. This is the beginning of the web.   3 minutes

STEPS: 6. After catching the ball of yarn, this person shares his response. Again the response is recorded on the flip chart. This toss, share and record process continues until everyone has had a chance to share. Be sure that everyone holds on to the yarn as he tosses the ball to insure that the web of celebration develops. 2 minutes per person

7. After everyone has shared, ask the last person to toss the ball of yarn back to you to complete the web. Note the variety of comments by quickly reviewing the flip chart pages. Ask people to observe the interconnectedness in the web of celebration. 5 minutes

VARIATIONS: An optional step is to use the web to model finding "hidden resources" by tightening the team connection. When the web is complete, ask the person to whom you first threw the yarn to pull it tightly between you and him. Then direct the person to whom he threw the yarn to do the same. Continue this progressive tightening until it is your turn to tighten the yarn between you and the last person who threw it to you. Note the quantity of extra yarn. Explain that this extra is representative of the extra time, money and energy the team can find as they continually tighten their team connection through effective decision making.

If the team is larger than 20 divide them into pairs or trios. Designate one person from each small group as the one who sits in the chair. The other(s) stand behind that person. They compose one response that represents all of them and the person in the chair states their shared response when he catches the yarn.

If the team is larger than 20, divide them into two groups and give each a ball of yarn. The two groups complete the activity independently. It will be necessary to appoint a recorder for both groups. They record all responses from their group on their flip chart. The responses on the two flip charts can be compared.

```
FACILITATOR NOTES
```

Your consensus puzzle is nearly finished. There are only a few pieces left and you will find them in Chapter 7, Tips and Hints: Suggestions for Success. This chapter offers you ideas that will increase the effectiveness of your team's decision making efforts. You will also find some suggestions to help you prevent some problems and troubleshoot them if they arise.

PROCESS TOOLS: Key Conclusions

• Process tools support the sixteen steps in the five phases of consensus. These step-by-step activities are used by the team during the consensus process.

• A process script prepares the team for the consensus process.

• A process tool helps a team successfully complete a step during the consensus process.

• Teams should choose the tools that best meet their needs.

TIPS AND HINTS: SUPPORTING THE PROCESS

> **WHAT DOES THE FACILITATOR DO DURING THE CONSENSUS PROCESS?**
>
> **WHAT IS A GROUP MEMORY?**
>
> **WHAT DOES A RECORDER DO?**
>
> **WHAT HAPPENS IF WE CANNOT REACH CONSENSUS?**

It's Thursday again. Once more our team has just finished a meeting. This meeting was upbeat and positive. The team has assembled the consensus puzzle. Let's listen to the conversation of two team members as they leave.

"What a great meeting. Celebrating the success of our consensus decision is a real emotional boost."

"I agree. However, we would never have those successes if we didn't have Jill as a facilitator and Keith as a recorder."

"You're right. Jill keeps us on task and manages to make it safe for all of us to speak our minds. She even helps us have some fun in the process. Keith and the others who have served as recorders have done a great job keeping the group memory."

The team members' conversation in this scenario emphasizes the importance of having a *facilitator*, a *recorder* and a *group memory*. This chapter describes all three of these ideas and gives hints to help teams gain the maximum benefit from each. In addition, the chapter describes the role of the team leader during consensus and provides some suggested back-up strategies teams can use if they find themselves unable to reach a consensus decision on a specific situation.

Let's begin with the facilitator. . . .

FACILITATOR

The facilitator is a neutral person who "serves" the team by engineering a safe environment, plans and guides effective group process and helps the team make the maximum use of their meeting time. The following list notes the facilitator's responsibilities specific to guiding the consensus process. The list is sequential and is cued to various chapters in the book.

Facilitator Responsibilities

Prior to the meeting:
- Be sure all team members are informed of the time, place, and agenda.

Before working on a specific consensus decision:
- Explain the purpose of the facilitator.
- Guide a dialogue about why the team should use consensus. Information to help with this dialogue is in Chapter 2.
- Teach the definition of consensus and use the process scripts to help the team meet all the prerequisites described in Chapter 3.

During the process of reaching a decision by consensus:
- Note that there is a situation facing the team that seems to require a decision.
- Help the team apply the reality filter questions and impact filter questions described in Chapter 4 to determine if consensus is the appropriate decision process to be used to address this situation.
- Coach the team through the first four phases of consensus: **Preparing, Possibilities, Probing, Declaring**. These phases are described in Chapter 5.
- Determine which of the steps within these phases need to be completed by the team. These steps are listed and described in Chapter 5.
- Guide the team in the completion of the necessary steps. Tools to support this work are in Chapter 6.
- Help the team work through the fifth phase, **Doing**.
- Assist the implementation chair, the person who was appointed to monitor the actual *doing* of the decision, as he supports and evaluates the implementation. Also help the chair provide update reports to the whole team.

At the end of the process
- Guide the team in celebrating their successes. Facilitate a debriefing that will help them learn from any failures that occurred during the implementation of the decision.

Chapter 7: TIPS AND HINTS:

Here are some hints to help the facilitator as he fulfills these responsibilities.

<u>Effective Meeting Management</u>
- Use a variety of colored vis-a-vis pens and felt tip markers. This gives visual interest.
- Organize necessary materials and equipment in advance.
- Coordinate with the person responsible for scheduling meetings and preparing agendas so sufficient time is designated for working on the consensus decision.
- Work in tandem with the recorder to keep a group memory. This is described later in this chapter.

<u>Collaborative Mind Set and Attitude</u>
- Maintain objectivity and do not become emotionally involved.
- Do not give personal opinions about the decision.

<u>Emotionally Safe Environment</u>
- Do not evaluate comments by team members.
- Keep your talk to a minimum.
- Use a variety of strategies to insure equitable participation of all team members.
- Paraphrase team members' comments when appropriate.
- Listen accurately for the facts.
- Listen actively for feeling tones.

<u>Positive and proactive language</u>
- Ask questions that support win/win problem solving.
    "How could we have some of_____and some of_____?"
    "Who would like to suggest a solution?"
    "Who has some concerns?"
    "Is there anyone who cannot live with that solution?"
    "Can you live with that solution?"
    "Can you think of any changes that would address your concern?"
- Use well crafted questions to help a team keep making progress.
    "What's stopping us from making a decision?"
    "Who would be willing to meet and develop an alternative?"
    "What information do we need in order to move on?"
- Pose questions that help people understand the position of the person who does not agree with or support the option advocated by *most*.
    "What specifically bothers you?"
    "What would you add, modify or delete so you could support this option?"

Because the role of facilitator is critical to successful consensus, organizations should allocate time and money for training a group of people in facilitation skills. These people develop into a cadre of facilitators that various teams within the organization can call upon for their services.

GROUP MEMORY

A powerful tool for increasing a team's consensus efficiency is the group memory. The group memory is a written record of the main points of what is said during a meeting. This record is created in full view of the group on a flip chart pad or on large sheets of paper taped or pinned to the walls of the meeting room. All that is needed are a few marking pens, large sheets of paper (or flip chart and easel) and someone to serve as recorder. This low cost, easy to use strategy is an asset for the team in many ways. Group memory:

- provides a visual focus to help the team stay on task,
- "remembers" participants' ideas. Individuals don't have to hold on to all the information in their heads,
- assures that participants have been accurately heard,
- helps prevent needless repetition,
- provides an instant record of a meeting's content and process,
- increases the group's sense of accomplishment because they can see work completed,
- provides a written record of team decisions,
- promotes continuity from one meeting to the next,
- clarifies who is accountable for what by recording names, action items, and deadlines.

The following illustration shows how to index the group memory. Use large sticky-back labels to create permanent tabs to index dates of meetings, decisions made and the dates of the decision as well as unfinished business.

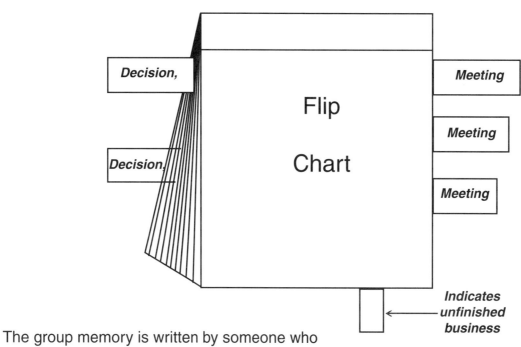

The group memory is written by someone who serves as a recorder and is a supplement to traditional minutes, not a substitute for them.

RECORDER

Because of the importance of keeping a group memory, team members will need to understand the role of recorder. This role is rotated among team members on a volunteer basis. During meetings the recorder writes key ideas, suggestions, concerns, comments, etc. on the flip chart that is designated as the group memory. Working in collaboration with the facilitator, he records basic ideas, not verbatim statements. He records the information clearly, legibly and concisely, checking  the accuracy of any paraphrasing or restating he has done. He also stops several times during the meeting to check the accuracy of what he has written. If the pace of the team conversation is faster than his ability to record, he should ask for help.

The following list provides some hints to help the person who serves as recorder.
- Use a variety of colored felt tip pens to color code different kinds of information.
- Underline important points for emphasis.
- Number all sheets of the group memory.
- Circle key ideas or statements.
- Use arrows, stars, and other symbols.
- Make the words an inch to an inch and a half high.
- Store the group memory in a consistent location known by all team members.

LEADER

The leader is the "sponsor" of consensus. He models his belief in the process by his commitment to learning the process and his active participation as one equal voice when the team makes consensus decisions. He also holds himself and all the team members accountable for honoring the group agreements and following the process.

As the team prepares for consensus the leader:
- Clarifies which decisions he will continue to make,
- Schedules time for the team to study the definition and answer the prerequisite questions,
- Appoints a facilitator to guide the process,
- Allocates the resources necessary to support learning and using consensus,
- Participates as a team member in the study of consensus.

During the consensus process the leader:
- Clarifies the team's authority to make the final decision relative to this situation,
- Provides information about any parameters relative to the situation,
- Participates as an equal member in all five phases of the consensus process,
- Provides support for the facilitator,
- Helps the team continue to gather information they need to make a well informed decision,
- Provides supervision to resolve concerns if a team member refuses to *gift* support after that person has had a reasonable opportunity to influence a decision and *most* has been reached,
- Provides feedback, if requested by the facilitator, if someone tries to sabotage a decision,
- Acts as a back-up source for a decision if the team cannot reach consensus and this is the predetermined strategy (see below).

The leader is a subtle, yet essential player in the process of consensus. His responsibilities and potential for positively influencing the process are great. As he "walks the talk" of consensus he helps the team learn the language and skills of consensus decision making.

BACK-UP STRATEGIES

Now let's assume that as a result of reading and using the information in this chapter your team enjoys the services of a skilled facilitator. Team members confidently and willingly volunteer to serve as recorder to keep the group memory. The team has mastered the content in the previous chapters and knows the answers to **why**, **what**, **when** and **how**. With all these positive conditions there still may be a time when the team cannot reach consensus. If and when this happens, it is important to be able to choose and apply a back up strategy. A team could:
- Submit the decision to a majority vote,
- Table the decision,
- Have the leader make the decision,
- Have a specified individual other than the leader make the decision,
- Delegate the decision to a committee or task force,
- Have those who support the decision pilot implementation for a trial period.

It is important to share these back up strategies with your team prior to a time when they need to use one. It might even be helpful to have them prioritize the strategies beginning with the one they would most prefer using to the one they like the least. Then, when the need for back-up occurs you can check the first strategy and if it fits the decision, you guide the team in the use of that strategy. Checking the fit is important because not all strategies will work with all decisions.

It is important to have the back-up options in reserve, but you will find they are rarely used. In our experience with consensus we find that if the team has studied the content, practiced the strategies and followed the five phases and the necessary steps, they will be able to reach authentic consensus.

Our work with teams has provided us with a living laboratory and the opportunity to study the dynamics of teamwork. When the team has the advantage of working with the support of a skilled facilitator and the team's work is visually supported by a group memory, the consensus process is always more effective and efficient. When the team has the guidance and example of strong leadership, a leader who understands his dual role as authority figure and participant in the process, the consensus process is likewise strengthened.

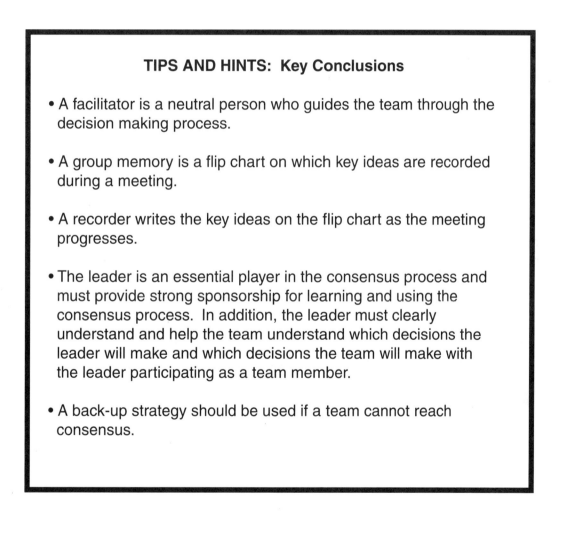

TIPS AND HINTS: Key Conclusions

- A facilitator is a neutral person who guides the team through the decision making process.

- A group memory is a flip chart on which key ideas are recorded during a meeting.

- A recorder writes the key ideas on the flip chart as the meeting progresses.

- The leader is an essential player in the consensus process and must provide strong sponsorship for learning and using the consensus process. In addition, the leader must clearly understand and help the team understand which decisions the leader will make and which decisions the team will make with the leader participating as a team member.

- A back-up strategy should be used if a team cannot reach consensus.

The consensus puzzle is complete! You have the four corner pieces, edges, and the middle pieces assembled. Your puzzle now matches the picture on the box lid. That picture shows your team efficiently and effectively reaching consensus.

We are convinced that it is a critical challenge for all teams to understand the consensus process and be prepared to use powerful strategies as they make important decisions. We enjoyed thinking about this challenge through the metaphor of a puzzle. We hope you found this puzzle metaphor a helpful and interesting support as you and your team strengthened and polished your consensus skills. Our greatest satisfaction is knowing our work has made a positive contribution to the effectiveness of teams. As we work face-to-face with teams we see strong evidence that our ideas on consensus really do help teams.

Because you picked up and read this book, you must have a similar commitment to increasing the effectiveness of team decision making. We hope that **Putting Sense Into Consensus** has answered your questions about consensus, validated your existing wisdom and skills, and added new insights, strategies and tools.

We would be delighted to know how this book worked for you and hear your ideas. Please feel free to email us with your comments.

Connie Hoffman   hoff@aa.net
Judy Ness   ness@aa.net

GLOSSARY

Beliefs   Foundation values essential to successful consensus.

Consensus   Consensus is a decision that has been reached when *most* members of a team agree on a clear option and the *few* who oppose it think they have had reasonable opportunity to influence that choice. All team members agree to support the decision.

Criteria   A judgment or rule used for evaluating something.

Facilitator   A neutral person who creates a safe environment, plans and guides effective group process.

Few   The percentage of team members whose opinion about a decision is different than the opinion held by the *most*.

Gifting   The act of stating a team member's willingness to support the implementation of a decision.

Goal   What a team wants to accomplish by a specific decision.

Group Memory   A written record of the main points of what is said during a meeting.

Impact Filters   Factors that indicate the significance of the effect of a decision on team members and on the work of the team. The presence of an impact filter indicates a strong need for a consensus decision.

Levels of Support   A framework of four categories of support (minimal, moderate, proactive and maximum) that allows team members to choose how much support they will *gift* to help implement a team decision.

Most   The minimum percentage of team members present at a meeting that must agree or disagree with an option to be able to say a decision has been reached.

Option   Something the team could do that is likely to produce the outcomes they desire from the consensus decision.

Parameter   Boundaries within which the team must work.

VISTA Associates
© 1998

Phases	A phase is a major part of the consensus process. There are five sequential phases:
	    Preparation--clearly stating the specific situation that will be the focus of the consensus process,
	    Possibilities--generating a variety of options or solutions to the situation,
	    Probing--checking individual opinions, "taking the pulse of the team" about the options in order to eliminate and prioritize options,
	    Declaring--stating the final decision reached by the team,
	    Doing--planning and completing the implementation of the team's decision.

Prerequisites	Questions for the team to answer prior to using consensus to ensure a successful consensus process.
Process Script	A step-by-step sequence to use when teaching a key concept or strategy to a team.
Reality Filters	Practical conditions that must exist for the team to choose consensus as the appropriate decision making method.
Recorder	A person who volunteers to write the key ideas, suggestions, concerns, comments, etc. on a flip chart designated as the group memory.
Responsibilities	The specific behaviors a team member is expected to use when working with fellow team members.
Rights	Specific expectations a team member can assume will be met as he works with fellow team members.
Situation Statement	A statement describing an issue that requires a decision.
Sabotage	Overt or covert interference with the implementation of a decision.
Steps	Specific actions taken by the team during each of the five phases. There are a total of 16 steps.
Support	The act of a team member doing his part to implement a team decision.
Tool	A sequenced activity that supports the completion of one of the steps of the five phases of consensus.
Vote	A stated choice between or among options that results in a team decision. A majority vote is 51% or one over half.

TRAINING AND TEAMBUILDING RESOURCES

In our consulting practice we provide a variety of training sessions to help teams gain skill and proficiency with the process of consensus. Some are overview sessions, others are more in-depth study and practice opportunities and still others are training of trainers sessions.

Training:

Putting Sense into Consensus: An Introduction and Overview
In this one day seminar we introduce people to the process of consensus decision making. They examine the **Why** and **What** of consensus and practice strategies for helping teams meet the prerequisites that result in a workable, practical definition that will guide the consensus process for the team. We also briefly overview the five phases and the sixteen steps.

Putting Sense into Consensus: An In-Depth Study
During this two day seminar we introduce people to the process of consensus decision making. Participants examine the **Why** and **What** of consensus and practice strategies for helping teams meet the prerequisites that result in a workable, practical definition that will guide the consensus process for the team. After studying the five phases and steps they participate in a "learning by doing" simulation of a consensus decision.

Putting Sense into Consensus: A Training of Trainers
This is a five day session during which we help participants learn the **WHY? WHAT? WHEN?** and **HOW?** of consensus. In addition, they learn the facilitation skills necessary for guiding the process of consensus. During the first three days they learn the content in a lab environment as they practice making a consensus decision. They then return to their work place and use the information to guide their team through the consensus process. Approximately a month later they return for the last two days.   During these days they participate in problem solving their concerns about the process and fine tuning their skills. They also learn how to train other members in the organization to be a facilitator of the process.

Putting Sense into Consensus: Customized Coaching
We are available as facilitators to organizations. In this role we coach a team through one of their actual consensus decisions. In the end they have a decision and they have learned the consensus process. We also help teams by watching their consensus process and giving them feedback on their strengths and we make specific suggestions on how they can strengthen their process.

VISTA Associates
© 1998

In addition to workshops on consensus we provide training and consulting on the following topics:
- the dynamics of effective teams - task productivity and trust relationships
- communication skills
- visioning and strategic planning
- shared decision making
- presenting skills
- facilitation skills for effective meetings and team learning

Teambuilding Resources

We have written other books that may be a resource for you and your teams. These include:

Tips and Tools for Trainers and Teams
This book is a collection of powerful and proven strategies you can use to build a team into a community of learners, support effective processing of information and provide for debriefing and celebration. Each strategy is fully scripted and includes all necessary worksheets and transparency black line masters.

Putting Power and Pizazz into Presentations
This resource provides suggestions for planning the delivery of information so your message has power and pizazz. It includes a checklist of survival supplies for anyone who leads a group; transparency blackline masters that can be used for any session to share agendas, state objectives, gather expectations, announce breaks, set time limits for activities, focus closure and much more.

Balancing the Head and the Heart: Communication for Teams
Here is everything you need to conduct a one day training that will help your team resolve the common communication problems of hidden agendas, decisions based on assumptions, a few voices dominating discussions and more. This resource contains everything you need to deliver a full day training session that will give you maximum training payoff for a minimum dollar investment.

As this *Putting Sense into Consensus* book goes to press we are working on a book of additional process scripts and tools. This book will add variety and flexibility to your "how to do consensus" repertoire.

In addition to the resources described above we have sets of transparency masters following various themes and an interesting collection of training aids. If you would like a catalogue of these materials email us and we will send one to you. Our address is printed on this computer screen.

Order Form

Send order to: *VISTA* **Associates**

5417 Orca Drive N.E. Tacoma, WA 98422

Fax: (253) 952-5426

	Price	Quantity	Total
Putting Sense Into Consensus	$26.50 1-9 copies $23.00 10 + copies		
Tips and Tools for Trainers and Teams	$55.00		
Putting Power and Pizazz into Presentations	$47.50		
Balancing the Head and the Heart: Communication for Teams	$85.00		

If you would like our complete catalog, check here and complete the address information below.

Yes, send me your complete catalog!

Product Total
WA residents add 8.4% sales tax
Total Amount

Ship to:
Name_____

Organization_____

Address_____

_____

Phone:_____
Fax:_____

Bill to:
_____

_____

_____

_____

Phone:_____
Fax:_____

Payment Information: Check Enclosed:_____ Purchase Order #_____

YES! I am interested in more information about your training components and facilitation services. Please contact me:

name: _____

phone number: _____

email address: _____